Alan Maley's 50 Creative Activities

Cambridge Handbooks for Language Teachers

This series, now with over 50 titles, offers practical ideas, techniques and activities for the teaching of English and other languages, providing inspiration for both teachers and trainers.

The Pocket Editions come in a handy, pocket-sized format and are crammed full of tips and ideas from experienced English language teaching professionals, to enrich your teaching practice.

Recent titles in this series:

Grammar Practice Activities (Second edition)
A practical guide for teachers
PENNY UR

Vocabulary Activities
PENNY UR

Classroom Management Techniques
JIM SCRIVENER

CLIL Activities
A resource for subject and language teachers
LIZ DALE AND ROSIE TANNER

Language Learning with Technology
Ideas for integrating technology in the classroom
GRAHAM STANLEY

Translation and Own-language Activities
PHILIP KERR

Language Learning with Digital Video
BEN GOLDSTEIN AND PAUL DRIVER

Discussions and More
Oral fluency practice in the classroom
PENNY UR

Interaction Online
Creative Activities for Blended Learning
LINDSAY CLANDFIELD AND JILL HADFIELD

Activities for Very Young Learners
HERBERT PUCHTA AND KAREN ELLIOTT

Recent Pocket Editions:

Penny Ur's 100 Teaching Tips
PENNY UR

Jack C. Richards' 50 Tips for Teacher Development
JACK C. RICHARDS

Scott Thornbury's 30 Language Teaching Methods
SCOTT THORNBURY

Alan Maley's 50 Creative Activities

Alan Maley

Consultant and editor: Scott Thornbury

CAMBRIDGE
UNIVERSITY PRESS

CAMBRIDGE
UNIVERSITY PRESS

University Printing House, Cambridge CB2 8BS, United Kingdom

One Liberty Plaza, 20th Floor, New York, NY 10006, USA

477 Williamstown Road, Port Melbourne, VIC 3207, Australia

314–321, 3rd Floor, Plot 3, Splendor Forum, Jasola District Centre, New Delhi – 110025, India

79 Anson Road, #06–04/06, Singapore 079906

Cambridge University Press is part of the University of Cambridge.

It furthers the University's mission by disseminating knowledge in the pursuit of education, learning and research at the highest international levels of excellence.

www.cambridge.org
Information on this title: www.cambridge.org/9781108457767

First published 2018

20 19 18 17 16 15 14 13 12 11 10 9 8 7 6 5 4 3 2 1

A catalogue record for this publication is available from the British Library

ISBN 978-1-108-45776-7 Paperback
ISBN 978-1-108-45777-4 Apple iBook
ISBN 978-1-108-45778-1 Google ebook
ISBN 978-1-108-45780-4 Kindle ebook
ISBN 978-1-108-45779-8 eBooks.com ebook

Contents

Thanks

My special thanks go to my editor, Alison Sharpe, for her meticulous attention to detail and her creative suggestions.
Alan Maley

Acknowledgements

Unless otherwise attributed, all creative writing texts have been written by the author, Alan Maley.

The authors and publishers acknowledge the following sources of copyright material and are grateful for the permissions granted. While every effort has been made, it has not always been possible to identify the sources of all the material used, or to trace all copyright holders.

If any omissions are brought to our notice, we will be happy to include the appropriate acknowledgements on reprinting and in the next update to the digital edition, as applicable.

Alan Maley for the text on pp. 21–22 from *Campbell's Crossing and Other Very Short Stories* by Alan Maley, published by Penguin Books Ltd. Copyright © 1995 Alan Maley. Reproduced with kind permission of Alan Maley; Michael Swan for the poem 'The Panther' on pp. 103–104 translated from 'Der Panther' by Rainer Maria Rilke. Copyright © Michael Swan. Reproduced with kind permission of Michael Swan.

Why I wrote this book

Creativity is widely regarded as a desirable quality in many fields. Yet for all the talk of creativity, there is relatively little of it to be found in educational contexts. I passionately believe creativity to be central to learning, including language learning, so this book is intended to offer, in however small a way, some resources for teachers who are interested in implementing more creative activities in their classes.

What do we mean by creativity?

In practice, creativity proves more difficult to define than we might expect. Amabile, one of the leading writers on creativity, affirms, 'a clear and sufficiently detailed articulation of the creative process is not yet possible' (1996). Yet we readily recognize creativity, even if we cannot define it. One problem is that creativity seems to be a cluster of attributes rather than a single quality: it comprises core ideas such as 'making something new', 'perceiving old things in new ways', 'finding new connections', 'being open to new insights' or 'evoking pleasurable surprise' (Maley 2003). Creative ideas also seem to need validation as relevant to a particular field: it is not enough to create something new – it also has to be seen as valuable. However, for practical purposes Kaufman and Sternberg (2007) offer a good working definition:

'First, those ideas must represent something different, new or innovative. Second, they need to be of high quality. Third, creative ideas must also be appropriate to the task in hand. Thus a creative response to a problem is new, good, and relevant.'

Why is creativity considered valuable?

Why is creativity perceived as desirable in our field of language learning and teaching? Clearly, language itself is inherently creative: we constantly coin new utterances. Anything which supports this is to be welcomed. Many people cite the power of creativity to arouse motivation and to sustain self-esteem among both students and teachers. The fact of making something original in another language is deeply satisfying. Activities involving creativity also seem to encourage risk-taking and spontaneity, and to free up inhibitions, which allow students to draw on the full range of their abilities. Such activities also seem to be more lively, more enjoyable and more conducive to a good classroom 'atmosphere'.

Many educational thinkers (Holt 1995) believe that children are naturally creative, and are educated out of creativity by the schooling they receive. Anything we can do to preserve innate creativity is to be welcomed. There is a widespread belief that creativity is a quality reserved for specially gifted people, like artists, musicians and poets. But we need to distinguish here between *big-C creativity* and *small-c creativity*. Big-C creativity (sometimes called *H* or *historical creativity*) refers to those who make highly original breakthroughs in their field – the Einsteins and Picassos of history. Small-c creativity (sometimes called *P* or *personal creativity*) refers to acts which are breakthroughs in the personal development of a person – for example when a child writes her first poem. These are things which have been done before by others but are original for the individual concerned.

We should also consider the long-term effects on both students and teachers of engagement with creative processes and outcomes. Arguably, one of the major benefits of such an approach is the formation of enduring attitudes among both students and their teachers – a more critical and exploratory mind-set, receptive of new ideas and alert to new ways of doing things.

Equally importantly, a more creative attitude is a good way for teachers to counter the growing culture of educational control. 'Education' dominated by measurement, standardized textbooks, curricula, checklists and examinations, makes it increasingly difficult for teachers to exercise their own judgement. Anything we can do to restore freedom of action to teachers is surely to be encouraged.

This book

I distinguish between creative products and the creative processes which give rise to them. So the activities on offer here will focus in varying degrees both on the creativity of inputs and products, and on the processes which help stimulate creativity.

Many of the activities favour more aesthetic modes of expression, such as the visual arts, music, drama and voice-work, and literature. Inputs like these are, of course, inherently creative anyway.

One of my main reasons for presenting them here is that they are attractive to students because of their intrinsic creative appeal. They are therefore ripe for exploitation as teaching material. They also present a greater diversity of modes of input.

Diversity of processes is also desirable because it helps sustain continued interest. But it is also important because it can offer something for all kinds of learner, including those with a preference for visual, for auditory, for physical movement and for tactile, as well as for purely logical kinds of material.

Quite a lot of current language teaching tends to concentrate on the cognitive aspects of language, leaving little room for exploring the affective dimensions. This is reflected in the fact that they are seriously under-represented in most standard course-book materials. The ideas presented are intended to offer something a little more stimulating and enjoyable.

Processes for generating creativity

I believe that we can facilitate creativity, even if we cannot directly teach it. So the activities draw upon a set of generic processes which can be applied to many different kinds of inputs. These ideas are based on a distillation of some of the work done in creativity studies. They offer a partial answer to the question, 'How do we generate new ideas?' They include:

- Using *the bi-sociative/random principle*, where we bring together unrelated items to spark new ideas (Koestler 1989).
- Working with repetition and reformulation to do old things in new ways and to re-fashion existing material into new forms. Using *the game/play principle*, involving us in 'messing around' with language in unconventional ways (Bateson and Martin 2013).
- Applying heuristics (rules of thumb), such as 'Do the opposite', to provoke creative responses (Fanselow 2012).
- Using the power of comparison, including metaphor, to look at familiar things in new ways.
- Exploring techniques such as brainstorming to generate new ideas.
- Using activities based on memories and memorization as a springboard.
- Using activities which involve physical movement (Ratey and Hagerman 2010).
- Applying *the withhold information principle* to engage the mind in supplying missing information.
- Using *the constraints principle* both as a challenge and as a support for creative outcomes (Boden 1992, Maley and Peachey 2015).

The combined effect of these principles is to provide a kind of creative toolkit for teachers which they can apply in their own ways. But we should not regard these activities as sure-fire recipes, they are ideas for further development.

What about level?

Most of these activities can be done at a variety of levels or can be adapted to different levels – both cognitively and linguistically. That is why I do not specify level. Teachers will adapt and work WITH these ideas, not necessarily TO these ideas. I don't see it as my business to know what every teacher knows far better than me – the chemistry of their class. I have grouped the activities into 5 main sections to facilitate access: *A: Creative Writing, B: Working with Music and Sound, C: Working with Drama and the Voice, D: Playing with Language* and *E: Hands-on Activities*. The activities are not in any particular order of difficulty, so teachers are encouraged to begin by choosing any activity which they feel would work well in their class, and progressively to try out others as they and their students gain in confidence.

The Creative Teacher

The activities are aimed at students learning together. But in using them, I hope that teachers too will be stimulated to explore more creative ways of doing things. Creative teachers of language know that it is not just a matter of teaching tenses, article usage, grammatical forms, vocabulary, etc. It is the beauty of the harmonious interlocking of complex systems that matters. It is an important part of the teacher's role to establish a learning community where error is not stigmatised, where learners are encouraged to take risks, where there is a maximum degree of freedom of choice, where there are learning challenges which are attainable and where there is a spirit of cooperation and trust between learners and between learners and teacher. To achieve this, teachers need to develop a creative stance as persons as well as developing creative attitudes and techniques. This can be done, though relatively little is on offer in formal training programmes. One source of ideas is Maley and Kiss (2017). I hope that by using some of the ideas in this book teachers will be encouraged to extend their creative range. There are additional references at the end of many activities for sourcing ideas.

Amabile, T. M. (1996) *Creativity in Context*. Colorado: Westview Press.

Bateson, P. and Martin, P. (2013) *Play, Playfulness, Creativity and Innovation*. Cambridge: Cambridge University Press.

Boden, M. (1992) *The Creative Mind: Myths and Mechanisms*. London: Abacus.

Fanselow, J. (2012) *Breaking Rules*. CreateSpace Independent Publishing Platform.

Holt, J. (1995) *How Children Fail*. Boston, MA: da Capo Press.

Kaufman, J. C. and Sternberg, R. J. (2007) Resource review: Creativity. *Change*, 39: 55–58

Koestler, A. (1989) *The Act of Creation*. London: Arkana/Penguin.

Maley, A. (2003) 'Creative approaches to writing materials'. In Tomlinson, B. (ed) *Developing Materials for Language Teaching*. London: Continuum.

Maley, A. and Kiss, T. (2017) *Creativity in Language Teaching: From Inspiration to Implementation*. London: Palgrave Macmillan.

Maley, A. and Peachey, N. (eds) (2015) *Creativity in Language Teaching*. London: The British Council.

Ratey, J. J. and Hagerman, E. (2010) *Spark: How exercise will improve the performance of your brain*. London: Quercus.

A: Creative Writing

This section offers activities which promote various kinds of creative writing, using a variety of stimuli, such as close observation, visuals, verbal manipulation and creative language use in the environment.

1   In the Distance: By My Feet

> This activity relates to the importance of close observation, which is one of the recurrent themes in this book. Noticing things is one of the key factors in creativity and indeed of language.

Introduce the activity by having a class discussion about the visual features which can help us to distinguish between one object or image and another. This would include: shape, size, height, distance, colour and tone, clarity of definition, texture, etc. Encourage students to be as specific as possible and to produce examples.

Explain that you will be taking students outside the classroom to an open area where there are long views. If possible, this should be to an area of natural beauty like a National Park but it could be in a smaller park in the city or any area of open ground, like a sports field. If it is not practicable to take the students very far, you can still use the playground or car park as long as there is a field of vision. You can even do this inside the classroom, asking students to do a 360 degree trawl and then to focus on their own desk. One other alternative is to use a picture with long vistas and detail in the foreground.

Students choose a place to stand, then look at the most distant place at the limit of their vision. They note down what they can see. They then turn a quarter-circle to their right, and do the same again. After that, they turn through the remaining two quadrants, taking notes as they go. Now ask them to turn their attention to what is closest to them – things near their feet. Again they turn through 360 degrees, making notes as necessary.

Back in the classroom, collect feedback on what students saw and noticed both far and near. If you want a more explicit language focus, this is a good time to draw attention to the order of adjectives before a noun. For example: *A line of low, stunted, lime-green willows, shrouded in mist.* What is the best order of adjectives?

Now ask students to choose one image from the distance and one from close to. They then write a few sentences which somehow create a connection between the two images. Their sentences should depict sharp visual images. These can then be worked up as a short prose poem.

An example from my own observation on a walk:

> Across a small lake, I notice the low line of willows (see above). I am standing on the shore of the lake and all around my feet there are wood chippings from a big willow tree which has recently been cut down. They look like the orange teeth of a dragon, or pieces of cheese rind, or the scales of a gigantic fish…

It is important to leave time for ideas to cook. For example, in the images above, I first thought of dragon's teeth and fish scales. In the writing, it seemed better to give the scales to the dragon and forget about the fish. I then thought of a dragon with teeth like a chain saw and I linked this with the distant willows, which may be eaten next! So I put the images together:

> The chain-saw dragon is hungry
> His orange scales litter the ground
> Where he has fed.
> Across the misty lake
> A line of willows crouches
> Hoping to escape his attention.

Students share their work and improve it if possible. Make sure it is exhibited as a wall display. Encourage students to illustrate their work, either manually or using computer graphics.

2 | Growing Stems Into Poems

> Here students revise and rehearse grammatical structures
> they have been taught in a light-hearted way that encourages
> them to introduce a note of fantasy and humour.

In this activity, students use grammatical stems to develop short poems.
A stem is the first part of a grammatical pattern, which students then
complete. For example:

I used to ... But now I ...

I love ... But I hate ...

Will you ...? Yes, I will./No, I won't.

All grammatical stems lend themselves to working in this way, so they
can be used with students at any proficiency level. You can choose
stems based on grammatical structures they are working on at the time.
Furthermore, writing simple poems like this also involves students
in multiple repetition, which is largely unconscious, and therefore
not tedious.

You need to explain how stems work, then demonstrate by developing a
short poem, eliciting the content to grow the stem. For example:

Will you ... (do something for me)?
Will you sit with me?	Yes, I will.
Will you talk to me?	Yes, I will.
Will you let me buy you a coffee?	Yes, I will.
Will you let me drive you home?	Yes, I will.
Will you come to my party?	Yes, I will.
Will you dance with me?	Yes, I will.
Will you marry me?	NO, I WON'T. I'm married already.

Then choose a stem you want them to work with. In pairs, students
try to find as many ways of completing the stem as possible. They then
try to arrange the sentences into a short poem as in the example. They

should try to make the last line humorous or striking in some way – by breaking the stem pattern.

When they have finished, pairs form groups of four and share their work. Groups then perform their poems for the class. (See **25 Performing Texts** for ideas.) Here is an example based on the request pattern and response: *Please* (+ do something). *I've already* … .

> Please clean your teeth.
> I've already cleaned them.
> Please wash your hands.
> I've already washed them.
> Please do your homework.
> I've already done it.
> Please turn off your phone.
> Oh, Mum …!

The idea of performing such short texts, which capture the rhythm of everyday speech, was first developed by Carolyn Graham. She called them jazz chants. Not all jazz chants are based on stems – sometimes they are more like substitution tables. For example:

I told you not to do it but you did it again (say, eat, buy, touch, drink, go there, come here, etc.).

One stem poem which always sparks creative and humorous versions is: *If you were a …, you'd be …* . Tell students to think of someone they really like (or don't like). They then complete the lines according to their feelings, comparing the person to a variety of items. For example:

If you were a flower, you'd be (a lily).

If you were an animal, you'd be (a leopard).

You can continue with many additional items: *a fruit, a dance, a writer, a game, a tree, a drink, etc.*

As always, when students produce work, make sure it is displayed somewhere, on a wall board or on the class/school website.

Graham, C. (2006) *Creating Chants and Songs.* Oxford: Oxford University Press.

Poem From a Picture

> We often fail to notice the things around us. Here is
> just one idea to develop noticing, which can lead into a
> creative writing activity.

You need to find an art picture which is either very atmospheric
(*Nighthawks* by Edward Hopper is a good example) or full of detail
(Renoir, Degas, Manet and Seurat are good sources), or a portrait
of someone with a striking appearance (for example, any of the self-
portraits by Rembrandt), or puzzle pictures (like those of M.C. Escher),
or variations of famous pictures like the Mona Lisa or humorous lively
pictures like Beryl Cook's. It is easy to find these and many other art
pictures on any big search engine.

You may decide to discuss the picture with students, inviting questions
and ideas from them. Useful vocabulary will arise naturally as needed
– for colours, shapes, positions, actions, movement, facial expressions
and body positions, moods (happy, sad, etc.). If it seems helpful, you can
write some of this vocabulary on the board as a support. Alternatively,
you might ask the students to discuss the picture in small groups or
pairs. They note down things that catch their attention, and any words
or phrases which come to mind, or items of vocabulary they do not
know but need. But whichever you do, make sure they really look
closely at the picture, noticing all the details. One way of doing this is
to use Kipling's 'Six honest serving men': *what, where, when, how, why*
and *who* questions. Ask students to ask as many questions as they can
think of for each of the question words.

Individually, students then write a poem based on their picture (between
five and ten lines). There is no need for it to rhyme: what is important
is to capture striking details or impressions or thoughts or metaphors
which the picture gives rise to. In pairs, students then exchange poems
and discuss what each has written. You can then invite them to read
their poems aloud to the whole class, if they wish. Ask them to review

their poems as homework and to bring their edited versions to the next class. These can then be used to make a wall display, a small booklet or a web page. It is important that they publish/make public what they have written as it provides a great boost for self-esteem and future motivation. Students have always produced some highly original work in this activity, and when they have written something original once, it seems to unlock their willingness to try it again.

If your students enjoy this activity, repeat it occasionally. You can also set an assignment for them to search for a picture which they particularly like or find interesting. You can then save the pictures in a file and use some of them as input to the activity at a later date.

Goldstein, B. (2008) *Working with Images*. Cambridge: Cambridge University Press.

Grundy, P., Bociek, H. and Parker, K. (2011) *English Through Art*. Innsbruck: Helbling.

Keddie, J. (2009) *Images*. Oxford: Oxford University Press.

May, S. and Ruanglertbutr, P. (2016) *Inspired English: Creative Writing and Critical Thinking Through Art*. Sydney: Macmillan Education Australia.

4 **Visual Poem**

> One of the ways memory is coded is through visual
> images – of things, people, faces, places, objects, events.
> This activity uses visual memory to generate associated
> words. It then organizes the words into a shape merging
> the words and the image.

Start with a word likely to evoke a strong visual image. For example,
an animal, a close friend or relative, a teacher, a building. In this case,
we will use the word *tree*. Ask the students to think of a tree which has
special associations for them. It could be a tree they have seen on holiday
or on a walk, or one they pass every day on the way to school, or where
something important happened. Allow enough time for this, then ask
them to draw a sketch of the tree. This does not have to be a work of art,
a few simple strokes giving the overall shape of the tree is fine.

Then ask students to write down words they associate with the tree
they have chosen. For the example below these words sprang to mind:
*isolated, alone, lonely, ancient, bristly, gaunt, battered, damaged by fire,
wind, no branches, proud, high above, strong, a survivor, etc.* At this
stage you may need to offer help in finding vocabulary as needed. Some
of the standard tree lexis will be available to them – *trunk, branch, twig,
leaf, roots etc.* – but they may lack others.

When they each have a list of 10–20 words, ask them to write short
sentences incorporating some of their words. For example: *The tree
stands alone. It is ancient and battered by wind and rain and fire. etc.*
Six to twelve sentences will be enough. They then need to organise the
sentences into a kind of prose poem. For example:

The tree stands alone.
It is ancient and gnarled,
Battered by wind and rain,
Charred by fire.

Yet still it stands proud –
Its branches are lopped off
But life still throbs in it.
Clumps of bristly leaves
Decorate its trunk in spring –
Birds come to nest.

Allow time for this. Students need to find exactly what they want to say, then formulate it accurately. Again you will need to help and advise them as they do this. Encourage them to edit and change what they have written – not to be satisfied with the first draft.

Each student then needs a piece of A4 paper. They draw the outline of their tree based on the sketch they did earlier. Make sure this takes up the whole of the sheet – no cramped little items in a corner. They then write their poem inside the shape of the tree, where possible using the shape creatively to fit the words. They may decide to edit some more at this point.

Ask them to share what they have done with classmates, and arrange a display of the work for everyone to see. Publishing their work gives it high face validity and enhances motivation, so it is important not to leave this stage out.

You might use this activity as the warm-up or introduction to a unit of work about trees (or whatever the subject chosen), before moving on to more formal activities. Alternatively, it could spark other ideas about using drawing and memory to stimulate the personalized and creative use of language.

Edwards, B. (2001) *The New Drawing on the Right Side of the Brain*. London: Harper Collins.

Milner, M. (2010) *On Not Being Able to Paint*. London: Taylor and Francis.

5 Prose Into Poetry

> How can we tell if something is a poem or not? One answer is to say that a poem is any text labelled as a poem – because once we are told a text is a poem, we tend to read it in a different way from plain prose.

The activity I am proposing here is deceptively simple. All it involves, superficially at least, is the copying out of a text. But in doing so, students must pay close attention, not only to the meaning of the text but also to the detail of how it is put together, the cadences of the sentences, to places which demand a longer or shorter pause, to the length of phrases and clauses within sentences, to how it would sound when spoken aloud. This means that they have to process the text at many levels, not simply at the level of comprehension. This involves multiple repetitions, even if these are mostly silent speech.

You need to find a text, preferably from a novel or short story. It should not be too long. Ideally it should be intrinsically interesting and contain some figurative language. The activity can be done in pairs or groups but I have found it is better done individually at first, with later discussion with a partner. Here is a sample text:

> … their father died. It was the time of the grape harvest. He had gone out after supper to check on the fermentation of the grapes in the vat. They found him floating in the vat, face downwards. He must either have had a heart attack or been overwhelmed by the powerful fumes. Whichever, he was well and truly dead, and there was nothing anyone could do about it. He was a brave man, respected by all, and regretted by all. He and his wife had survived many hardships together. But she could not bear to live alone. Within three months, she had followed her husband to the place where all sufferings cease. The two boys were left alone.

(from *The Man Who Talked to Trees* by A. Maley)

Read the text aloud to the class as it is printed above. Check if there are any comprehension problems. Then ask students to read it aloud to each other – also as a prose text. They should now work individually. Explain that they should write out the text as if it were a poem. Explain that they will have to decide where the line breaks come. Discuss some of the factors which will influence their choice. For example, they may feel it is natural to break a line after a grammatical chunk (phrase or clause), or to put words they think are especially important on a separate line for emphasis, or to give the poem a shape to reflect the meaning, or break the lines into stepped sequences. They may want to listen to how it sounds and break at places where there would be a natural pause.

Allow time for students to write out the text as a poem. Ask them to give it a title. In pairs, they then compare the ways they have chosen to display it and their titles. Then hold a class discussion. Were any of the poems identical? (The chances of this happening are infinitesimal.) What about titles? Ask for volunteers to read their poems to the class. How different did this sound from when they read the text as prose? Ask students to bring final copies to the next class and make a wall display of them.

Literature is not something remote from everyday language use – we find many instances of literary language in a wide range of non-literary texts – proverbs, aphorisms, graffiti, quotations, newspaper headlines, advertising slogans, book and film titles, shop signs, T-shirts, jokes, etc., as well as in everyday conversation. This playfulness is an important feature of language use.

Firstly, choose about five of the items listed below to discuss.

- *The minority is sometimes right: the majority is always wrong.* (Bernard Shaw quote. Intertextuality – referring to the popular saying: *The majority is always right.* Two parallel structures with contrasting elements: *minority/majority, right/wrong.*)
- *I am anonymous. Help me!* (Graffiti on a wall. Paradoxical joke: if I am anonymous, how can anyone help me?)
- *I'm not afraid of dying: I just don't want to be there when it happens.* (Woody Allen. Paradoxical joke.)
- *Failing Much Better Now.* (Newspaper headline. Word play. We expect *Feeling* but it uses *Failing.*)
- *Just as nice: at half the price.* (Supermarket ad. Two parallel phrases which rhyme and share the same stress/rhythm.)
- *Work is the curse of the drinking classes.* (Oscar Wilde. An example of metathesis, where two items are reversed. The reversed saying is: *Drink is the curse of the working classes.*)
- *Lunatic Fringe.* (Shop sign for a hairdresser. A pun. The phrase means 'a bit crazy' but also refers to a fringe of hair.)
- *Short cuts.* (Hairdresser shop sign. A pun on the phrase *short cuts* – a quick way to go somewhere.)
- *Invest your nest egg: Eggceptional returns.* (Rhyme – *invest/nest*, assonance of the /e/ sound. Word play – *eggceptional.*)
- *Meals on wheels.* (Name of a service delivering meals to old people. Internal rhyme.)

- *Tower of Pizza.* (Pizza restaurant. Pun on *The Leaning Tower of Pisa.*)
- *Journey's Friend.* (Sign on a railway station food outlet. Pun on the phrase *Journey's End.*)
- *Hare Brain: Tortoise Mind* (Book title. Two parallel phrases contrasting speed: *hare/tortoise,* and quality of thought: *brain/mind.*)
- *Feelin' cannelloni?* (Sign in Italian restaurant. Sound play: *cannelloni/kinda lonely.*)
- *Seoul Mate (Korean restaurant. Sound play: Seoul/soul.)*

Write your choices up on the board one by one without explaining them. Ask students what they think they might mean and where they might have come from (proverb, advertisement, headline, etc.). Then draw attention to the literary devices they are using (rhyme, rhythm, alliteration, assonance, repetition, parallelism, figurative tropes like metaphor, paradox, ambiguity, puns, metathesis, intertextuality, etc.). Because there is an element of surprise, we pay more attention to such uses of language.

The students now work in groups of three. Give each group four of the remaining items from the list, so that all the items are covered. Do not give them the explanations or sources. Allow about 15 minutes for them to discuss their items, suggest a possible source, and the devices being used. Then have a feedback session.

At the end of the session, either design a wall chart or open a special page on the class website where students can add new items as they find them in the coming weeks.

7 New Ways of Seeing

This is a powerful activity which helps students to really take time to get inside an object, and leads into creative writing.

Bring in a selection of interesting-looking stones. Alternatively, ask each student to bring a stone which interests them. Allow about ten minutes for students to look closely at their stone, noting down their observations in writing – colour, shape, texture, any unusual features like cracks, scratches or holes, etc. You may need to help out with vocabulary items here.

Then ask students to imagine that they are the stone. They should then write a short piece from the point of view of the stone. *What might the stone say about itself? What does it look like? Where has it come from? What has happened in its life so far? What does it enjoy most? What is it afraid of? What does it hope for in future?* They may find it useful to ask themselves the questions – *when, where, what, why, how* and *who*. For example, 'Where was I born?' In this way they will find more to say about themselves. Some students may wish to make a drawing of the stone to accompany what they have written. They then share what they have written in pairs. Finally have them make a wall display of their writings and drawings.

You can extend this activity in the next class by asking students to write about the same stone but from a third person perspective, for example by asking them to write a review of the stone as if it were a sculpture in an art gallery.

You can adapt this as a speaking activity too, where students tell the story of their stone, or develop a dialogue between two stones.

A good way to round off the activity is to collect all the stones and put them on a table. Students then have to come and find their stone, and explain to a partner how they recognized it.

You can use other objects in the same way, of course: leaves, flowers, buttons, keys, stamps, old coins, etc. John Fanselow has some interesting variations on this idea using postage stamps.

You can also give the activity a twist by asking students to look carefully at their own (non-dominant) hand. They then draw this hand. Having to make a drawing of something forces you to observe it in great detail. After that, they write a short poem about their hand. Encourage them to invent metaphors or similes: *My hand is like a starfish. My hand is a claw. My hand is five peninsulas stretching out from the mainland of my palm. My hand is like a flower, opening and closing its petals.* etc.

You can extend the idea of metaphors for an object, taking inspiration from Wallace Stevens' famous poem, *Thirteen Ways of Looking at a Blackbird*. Ask students to choose a very ordinary object, like a pencil, a book, a pair of scissors. They should then come up with four similes or metaphors for their object using the first person, followed by a comment or extension of the metaphor. For example, for a pen, *I am a torpedo full of words, soon I will explode on the page,* for a book, *I am a sandwich of ideas, open me and enjoy my flavour.* They then combine their images to form a four-line poem. This can be made into a riddle poem if they add a line at the end: 'So what am I?'.

Fanselow, J. (1992) *Contrasting Conversations*. New York: Longman.

8　Comparing Pictures

Comparison and contrast are powerful processes. Here we focus on pictures on the same theme.

Start by showing or distributing two pictures on the same subject. The following are readily accessible on search engines:

- Edward Hopper: *Automat* and *The Barber Shop*
- Thomas Gainsborough: *Mr and Mrs Andrews* and David Hockney: *Mr and Mrs Clark and Percy*
- Walter Sickert: *Ennui* and Edward Hopper: *Room in New York*

Individually, students make a list of all the differences they notice between the two pictures. Remind them of the possible features which can vary: foreground, background, position in the picture, number of people/objects, size, shapes, colours, light, type of clothing, facial expression, movement, visual focus, etc.

Students then work in pairs to compare the points they have listed. This will offer them many opportunities for using comparative forms.

Then remove the pictures. Individually, students draw one of the pictures from memory and from their notes. In pairs, they then compare their drawings with the originals.

Next, using their own drawing, students compose a short text using vocabulary they have noted during the earlier part of the activity. The text may be a short poem, a straight description, an entry in an exhibition catalogue. Here is an example based on Sickert's *Ennui*:

> Their marriage was once green.
> Now it is brown –
> Their whole world is brown and dull and dreary –
> There is nothing left to say.
> Life is one big yawn.

Finally, ask students to make a class display of the drawings along with the texts.

Working With Word Arrays 9

'Jumbled words' will be familiar to most language teachers. This activity takes the jumbled words idea a step further by making it possible for students to create texts of their own within a supportive framework.

To make a word array, you need a short text with many of the words in it repeated several times. Short texts of this kind are not very difficult to write or adapt (Szkutnik 1991). Here is an example (adapted from Szkutnik 1973):

He never gave me presents. He never wrote me letters. He never took me to concerts. He never spoke of love. We met in the carpark. I don't remember exactly what he said. He hardly spoke anyway. Now I don't even remember his face.

From this you can generate the following word array. It contains all the words from the text but if they are repeated, it still only uses them once in the array.

face	*he*	*we*	*don't*
letters	*never*	*presents*	*said*
concerts	*of*	*even*	*me*
now	*love*	*I*	*in*
remember	*carpark*	*took*	*gave*
wrote	*to*	*hardly*	*spoke*
his	*anyway*	*met*	*what*
	the		*exactly*

Note that you do not show the text to the students – only the word array.

To start with, students work on their own. Their task is to use the words in the word array to generate as many correct sentences in English as they can. They write these down. The rules are:

- students can only use words that are in the array. They cannot add new words.

- they cannot change the form of the words. For example, they cannot write *loves* – only *love*.
- they can use the words as many times as they like.
- they do not have to use all the words in the array – but it is better if they do.

The activity offers a degree both of support and of constraints: the words ensure that there will be some semantic threads which everyone will pick up on. At the same time, it leaves students free to construct their own meanings through the texts they create. Withholding the original text till the end generates a lot of interest and anticipation.

You need to allow students time to generate at least five or six sentences each. Monitor what they write and ask for some examples before moving on. They then share their sentences with a partner so that each pair can make a composite list of their sentences. Pairs then join to form groups of four, who again share their sentences and add the new ones. After this, again ask for examples. These may be very short: *He never spoke.* Or longer: *Anyway, I don't even remember the concerts he took me to, the letters he wrote, the presents he gave me.*

The groups now pool their sentences and use some of them to generate a new text – either a poem or a short narrative piece. For example: *We met. He gave me presents. He wrote me letters. He spoke of love. Now I don't even remember him.*

Again allow time for this. Ask groups to read their texts to the class, and ask them to make a wall display of them.

Finally, give out copies of the original text so students can compare it with what they wrote. One strength of the activity is that it can be done by students at many different levels. They will produce the sentences they are capable of, whatever their level.

Szkutnik, L. L. (1973) *Thinking in English*. Warsaw: Panstwowe Wydawnictwo Naukowe.

Szkutnik, L. L. (1991) *Lyrics in English for Comprehension and Interpretation*. Warszawa: Wiedza Powszechna.

Recipe Poems

Everyone is familiar with the genre of the recipe. In this activity we give the recipe for meals a creative twist by applying it to other domains by creating recipes for things like anger, disappointment, winter, poverty, drought, etc.

Begin by asking students what a recipe is and what kinds of language we can expect to find in recipes: ingredients, quantities and measurements, processes, outcomes, etc. You may want to bring in some actual recipes from cookery books, or ask your students to check them online using their smartphones. They can then work in pairs or small groups to brainstorm as many items of quantity/measurement they can think of. For example: *a teaspoonful, a cup of, a litre of, a pinch of, a slice of, a bunch of, a clove of* … . Write these up on the board under 'Measures'.

Then ask students to brainstorm as many of the verbs for processes commonly associated with recipes/cooking as they can. For example: *boil, beat, chop up, cut, fry, roast, serve up, simmer, steam, stir,* … . Write these up under 'Processes'.

Now explain that they will be writing a special kind of recipe – not for food. Either offer a choice of a few possible words, like *anger, flooding, peace, hope, vanity,* etc. or just give them one word you have chosen for them. In pairs, students then write a recipe poem of about ten lines relating to the theme word. Remind them to use measuring words and process verbs as appropriate. You may wish to offer an example, though this may not be necessary. Here is one possible example:

A Recipe for Drought
Take a plainful of dust,
Nine months-worth of sun,
A wind from the desert,
One cloudless sky,
Five dead cows,
Ten dried-up wells,
A child begging for food,

An old woman crying dry tears.
Mix them together
with a world full of indifference.
Cook for a year.
Serve up on Newsnight.

Set students a time limit. When time is up, they can compare their poems with other pairs. They may find they want to edit their work after this. If there is time, they can then read their poems to the rest of the class. Finally, get them to make a display of all their work so that everyone can read it.

A slightly simpler activity can also be effective. It involves writing a shopping list poem.

First, introduce the topic of shopping. Working in small groups, students produce a shopping list of about ten items. They will probably mention items such as:

a loaf of bread, a packet of tea, a kilo of potatoes, 500 grams of onions, a bottle of cooking oil, a bunch of flowers, a bag of peanuts, etc.

Make sure that students understand the difference between things which can be counted e.g. *five apples,* and those which cannot, e.g. *sugar, oil, bread, flour,* etc.

Now tell them that there is a magical supermarket where they can buy some of the human qualities they would like. Give a few examples to get them going. Solicit some more ideas from the class. For example:

A *pint of hope.*
A *packet of love.*
A *kilo of common-sense.*
A *bunch of memories.*
A *bagful of luck,* etc.

Students then work in small groups again to produce a shopping list poem which begins:

At the supermarket of dreams,
I need to buy:
A bunch of friends, etc.

Students then list items based on things they discussed above.

> One of the challenges for any teacher of language is how to provide input at a suitable level of challenge along with processes that will encourage students to engage actively with it. One way of doing this is to adopt a playful attitude which allows students to manipulate the language without fear of failure.

In this activity, students are asked to dig items out of one text and use them to write another. You need to select a text which is rich in evocative, striking language, as in the extract below. Allow time for students to read it and to ask for clarifications if necessary. Then ask them to underline five to eight words or phrases they find particularly striking. They should write these on a separate sheet of paper. Now collect up the original texts so that all they have to work with are the bits of language they have written down. Tell them that they must now use the language they selected as part of a new text. They must use all the words they chose but they can change their grammatical form (e.g. *cruel, cruelty, cruelly*). The idea is not to try to reconstruct the original but rather to construct a completely new text. In order to do this, students must deeply engage with the content and language of the text. (It may even be good to do the writing in a later lesson when they have forgotten the original text.)

His hands, resting lightly clasped on the table, were as powerful as ever. They made me shiver as I remembered what I had seen them do. Once they had picked up five small kittens. I had watched him put them in a sack, then calmly drop the sack into a tank of water. These hands had held the sack under water until the bubbles stopped. He had smiled his strange smile and said, 'Sometimes you have to be cruel to be kind.' But he looked as if he had enjoyed it.

I remembered thinking that I had never seen Alfred smile. I had never seen him angry either. And never heard him raise his voice.

In fact he never really showed his feelings. He smiled. But it was a pitiless smile. His smile was a mask. I had not realized what lay behind it.

(from *Alfred's Enigmatic Smile* by A. Maley in *Campbell's Crossing and Other Very Short Stories*)

Here is one list of possible fragments:

lightly clasped, five small kittens, his strange smile, cruel to be kind, a pitiless smile, a mask, never showed his feelings, until the bubbles stopped

A text which incorporates these linguistic 'organ implants' might be:

I watched him from my hiding place. First he drowned the five small kittens. He smiled until the bubbles stopped. It was a strange smile. He never really showed his feelings. Then he turned to the girl. 'You see,' he said. 'Sometimes you have to be cruel to be kind. Now it's your turn.' And he clasped her neck in his huge hands and slowly strangled her. And all the time he smiled his pitiless smile.

When students have finished, they exchange their texts with a partner. They read and comment on the texts, which they edit as homework. After you have checked their texts, hold a class feedback session and comment on some of the more interesting efforts. Then give back the original extract so that students can compare it with their own. Ask them to make a wall display of their texts with the original text in the middle and their texts arranged around it.

Making Metaphors

Language loves metaphors. The moment we create a
metaphor, bringing together two previously unrelated
words, we begin to look for connections. This is a very
simple but powerful activity where students make their
own metaphors and find a justification for them.

The word 'metaphor' can be off-putting. You can simply say 'unusual
comparisons'. Or, if it seems appropriate, explain briefly what a
metaphor is. You might choose to illustrate from a poem, like Alfred
Noyes' famous poem *The Highwayman*:

> The wind was a torrent of darkness among the gusty trees.
> The moon was a ghostly galleon tossed upon cloudy seas.
> The road was a ribbon of moonlight over the purple moor,
> And the highwayman came riding –
> Riding – riding –
> The highwayman came riding, up to the old inn-door.

The wind is not actually *a torrent of darkness*, nor is the moon a
ghostly galleon, nor the road *a ribbon of moonlight* but using these
comparisons makes the effect more striking and visual. That is how
metaphors work.

This is an adaptation of an activity by Jane Spiro (see the reference
below). First of all, either project or distribute this chart to students.

A	B
Hate	a brush
Love	a spoon
Marriage	a knife
Sleep	a banana
Disappointment	a bus
Hope	a screwdriver

Pride	a window
Justice	an onion
Work	a rope

Then ask everyone to write down three metaphors by combining any item from column A with any item from column B and joining them with *is*. Make sure to tell students that they cannot get this wrong. Whatever combination they come up with will be a metaphor.

Here are some examples:

- *Disappointment is an onion.*
- *Marriage is a banana.*
- *Hate is a screwdriver.*
- *Sleep is a window.*

Ask around the class to get a sense of what they have written. Stress that any item from one column can go with any item from the other. There are no right answers.

Then ask students to choose one of their metaphors and to write a poem of one or two lines which will help us to understand how the metaphor works. For example:

Sleep is a window –	Disappointment is an onion
When we sleep we open it	It looks good from the outside
To enter another world.	But when we peel it
	It makes us cry.

Students share their work, then prepare a wall display of their metaphor poems. It is really important to make public what they write, and not to display only the 'best' examples. Everyone should feel their work and effort has been appreciated, which helps build a sense of cooperation.

Duff, A. and Maley, A. (2007) *Literature*. Oxford: Oxford University Press.

Maley, A. and Duff, A. (1989) *The Inward Ear: Poetry in the Language Classroom*. Cambridge: Cambridge University Press.

Matthews, P. (1994) *Sing Me the Creation*. Stroud: Hawthorn Press.

Spiro, J. (2004) *Creative Poetry Writing*. Oxford: Oxford University Press.

New Headlines for Old

Headlines have to fit into a defined space on the page, catch the attention of readers, and convey the essence of the article which follows. In this activity, students are invited to have fun recombining headlines to produce some original new ones.

You need to make a collection of at least 20 headlines from English language newspapers. When choosing, you need to look out for headlines which can be conveniently syntactically divided. Very short ones, like *We Won!*, are not useful for this activity. But a headline like *Patience isn't always a virtue* can be divided into *Patience isn't // always a virtue* or *Patience isn't always // a virtue*. If you make this activity part of your repertoire, you will gradually build up, through trial and error, a collection of headlines which are guaranteed to produce interesting recombinations.

Here is a possible selection:

- *Hidden Camera Reveals Truth About Hospital Mismanagement*
- *Imagine What It's Like to be Homeless*
- *Women Reject Threats from Religious Families*
- *Princes Linked to Racing Fraud*
- *Kidnapped Model Found Alive in Australia*
- *Gone are the Days of Political Cooperation*
- *A Bold New Vision Brought to British Museum*
- *Mystery of Banker's Disappearance*
- *Kim Plays Poker with US: A Dangerous Game*
- *Tax-free Loophole Plugged at Last*
- *'It's Time to Go,' says Oscar-winning Actor*
- *The New Trend: House-husbands and Working Wives*
- *Caught on Camera: That Secret Kiss*

After distributing the list of headlines, discuss at least some of them with students. Are there words they do not know? What might the articles they belong to be about? Then show them how the headlines can be broken down in different ways, as in the example above.

Students then work in pairs to make some new headlines by combining parts of two headlines. Each pair should try to make up at least three new headlines. For example:

- *Hidden Camera Reveals That Secret Kiss*
- *Banker's Disappearance Linked to Racing Fraud*
- *'It's Time to Go,' Says US*
- *Kidnapped Model Found Alive in British Museum*
- *The New Trend: Threats from Religious Families*
- *Caught on Camera: House-husbands and Working Wives*
- *Gone are the Days of Racing Fraud*
- *Princes Linked to Banker's Disappearance*
- *House-husbands and Working Wives: A Dangerous Game*

Each pair joins another pair. They exchange and discuss the headlines they have created. Everyone then reports back to the class. They should suggest what the articles corresponding to their headlines might be about. Record any specially striking headlines on the board.

Keep a record of all the new headlines. In a later class, students can use this bank of materials to select lines which fit together into a headlines poem.

As a follow-up introduce Paul Dehn's poem *Gutter Press* (easily found on any search engine). This is very suitable for discussion of the issues around unethical journalism. It is also excellent as a performance poem.

Grundy, P. (1993) *Newspapers*. Oxford: Oxford University Press.

Sanderson, P. (1999) *Using Newspapers in the Language Classroom*. Cambridge: Cambridge University Press.

> Probably the best-known form of syllabic poetry is the haiku. But there are other types of poem which also depend on syllable counts, such as the Tanka and the Cinquain. One advantage of using these forms in the language classroom is that they impose tight constraints which force students to actively manipulate the language they have available.

You need to make sure students understand what a syllable is: a single vowel sound with or without a consonant attached. Give an example of a few haiku (five syllables in line one, seven in line two, five in line three).

On this old birch tree	(five syllables)
A solitary crow sits	(seven syllables)
Black eyes watching me.	(five syllables)

The importance of constraints cannot be over-emphasized. Having to work within 17 syllables (for haiku) means students have to stretch and re-arrange the language they have available until they find something that fits both their idea and the language used to express it.

But syllables are only one part of making a haiku. Usually haiku are about some aspect of nature. They are like a verbal snapshot of a moment of insight into life. They also depend on a moment of keen insight, which in its turn comes from close observation – often transforming something ordinary into something which provokes thought or emotion. This is why something like this, though it obeys the syllabic rules, is not really a haiku.

It's a lovely day.
I am enjoying myself.
I love my teacher.

You can ease students into writing haiku by providing the first two lines and asking them to write the third. Then give just the first line and they write the last two. Or the last two and they write the first. Once students are comfortable with the form, encourage them to write one of their own. First they need to find a 'haiku moment' based on close observation. If you can, take students outside. If not, distribute some ordinary objects and allow time for close observation before they write. They need to work within the constraints of the five-seven-five syllables. And usually the first two lines set the scene and the last line makes us sit up and take notice. They share what they have written with classmates.

Explain that the haiku developed into the Tanka by adding two more lines of seven syllables each. For example, we could add to the haiku above:

Suddenly it flaps its wings.	(seven syllables)
Terror: my heart stops beating.	(seven syllables)

Go on to discuss other forms of syllabic poetry, such as the Cinquain. This has five lines of two, four, six, eight, and two syllables respectively. Again there are rules:

Line 1: two syllables. States the topic.	*Babies:*
Line 2: four syllables. Adjectives describing topic.	*adorable,*
Line 3: six syllables. Verbs ending in *–ing*	*laughing, crying, wetting*
Line 4: eight syllables – feeling or observation	*but they become teenagers, then*
Line 5: Variant of or comment on line one.	*they're gone.*

Encourage students to experiment with other syllabic arrangements. For example, line one, one syllable, then line two, two syllables, line three, three syllables, up to line ten, ten syllables.

As with many of these activities, this one is best developed regularly during the course. It can be made into a mini-project to produce a small photocopied booklet of students' work.

B: Working with Music and Sound

All the activities in this section work with musical improvisation. Some use music as a stimulus for rhythmical movement. Some others lead from music into writing.

15 Rhythmic Clapping

> Rhythm and music are at the centre of spoken language.
> Many, perhaps all, students need to move, yet we expect
> them to sit immobile for quite long periods. There is now
> evidence which shows enhanced levels of brain activity
> accompany physical movement (Ratey and Hagerman 2010).

Clapping is a good way to get started. It is best if the students can
stand in a circle, facing inwards. Explain that they will be doing some
clapping games. There is an enormous variety of ways to use clapping,
so these are simply one possible selection. Designate one student to
start with a single clap, the person to the right continues, and the clap
travels all round the circle. The transitions between claps should be as
smooth as possible, with no hesitations. Repeat the activity going in
the opposite direction, speed it up. Then have two students start the
clap. They stand opposite each other on the two sides of the circle. One
claps to the right, one to the left. When the claps meet, the person in the
middle has to clap twice. Repeat the exercise. This time, when a student
claps, they say the name of the person receiving the clap, offering with
a gesture the name as a gift. Next, as a student claps they add words,
perhaps a simple exchange: *How ARE you?* (light, heavy, light). *I'm
FINE* (light, heavy). As they say the words, they clap the rhythm.

You can introduce a competitive element. Write up a list of ten words or
phrases on the board, possibly ones recently introduced in the coursebook.
They should have varied stress patterns. For example: *hot, banana, eleven,
sixteen, bread and butter, half past ten, microscopic, happy, tomatoes,
hamburgers.* In pairs, students take turns at clapping a word from the list.
The other student has to guess which word is being clapped. If there is
space, students can circulate, changing partners after each turn.

You can extend this to sentences. Write up about ten sentences, again
perhaps ones from the coursebook you are working with. *Peter doesn't
like hamburgers. Let's go to the cinema tonight. Can you lend me a*

pound? etc. Practise clapping these with the class. First, just clap them. Then clap adding the words. Students then work in pairs again, taking turns to clap one of the sentences from the list. If the student receiving a sentence identifies it, they have to clap it, then speak it.

Groups work on orchestrating short texts: first they clap the rhythm, then they speak along with the clapping. There are some suitable texts in Carolyn Graham's many books on jazz chants (see the reference below for an example).

You can then even work with longer texts like the one below. To do this, divide the class in two. One team claps the first half of the line, the second team the second half of each line. They then repeat the process and speak the lines as they clap.

Missing Person
Shirts in the drawer – unworn.
Clothes in the basket – unwashed.
Books on the shelf – unread.
Mails in the inbox – unanswered.
Money in the bank – unspent.
Bills on the desk – unpaid.
Envelopes on the floor – unopened.
Food in the fridge – uneaten.
Wine in the rack – undrunk.
Chances for a life – unlived.
Whereabouts – unknown.

This is another kind of activity which is ideally done regularly for a short time.

Graham, C. (1998) *Singing, Chanting, Telling Tales*. McHenry, IL: Delta Systems, Co. Inc.

Ratey, J. J. and Hagerman, E. (2010) *Spark: How exercise will improve the performance of your brain*. London: Quercus.

16 Vocal Tapestry

> Choral repetition is viewed as mechanical and de-motivating. However, we need to repeat language items many times before they are acquired. This activity solves this problem – by personalizing the language used, and framing the repetition as an aesthetic performance.

The basic idea is simple. Students work in groups of up to ten. Each student is given (or chooses) an item of language. This is *their* sound or word or phrase. No one else has it. It belongs to them. The aim of the group is to produce a kind of vocal tapestry by weaving together their voices – each group member repeating their item in various combinations. The aim is to make the performance as aesthetically pleasing as possible. The performance is limited to two minutes in length.

This can be done at many different levels. Here are some examples of language areas which can be practised in this way:

- Non-verbal vocalizations. We use a range of very useful non-verbal emoters – vocalizations to express, for example, pain (*Ouch!*), admiration (*Wow!*), disappointment (*Oooh!*), wonder (*Aaah! Ooo!*), relief (*Phew. Ouff!*), recognizing a mistake (*Whoops!*), getting attention (*Hey!*), pleasure (*Aaaaw!*), go away (*Shoo!*), we don't like you (*Boo!*), be quiet (*Shhh!*), I see (*Aha!*), now I get it! (*Ahaa!*), mock sadness (*Boo-hoo*). These emoters are culturally specific, so form an important part of what it is to sound English. Before starting the choral work, it is best to elicit/provide a list of these sounds.
- Phonemes. Allocate the vowel sounds of English, one per student. (e.g. /i/, /iː/, /æ/, /aː/, etc.) Include the diphthongs (/ei/, /ai/, etc.).
- Syllables. Syllables are made up of a consonant–vowel combination. e.g. *ba, fi, go*, etc. The more interesting ones are those with multiple initial consonant clusters, e.g. *spr-, str-, dr-, tr-*.

- Words. Rather than selecting words at random, it is better to work with semantic clusters. e.g. around theme words like *rain: wet, cold, drizzle, pouring, storm, umbrella, etc.* or words linked to a text they are studying, e.g. *Hamlet: to be, king, queen, prince, murder, revenge, doubt*, etc.
- Phrases. Again you can offer phrases which cluster around a semantic core, e.g. *We're late, Hurry up, We'll miss it, Aren't you ready yet?, It's always like this, Look at the time!, We'll never make it, Let's get going, Stop wasting time, I'm ready, what about you?, Come on for goodness' sake,* etc.

For all these areas, first allocate a sound, word or phrase to each student. Let them practise different ways of saying it. Groups then need some rehearsal time to work out the most effective way of weaving the repeated sounds together. Suggest they add gesture, facial expression or movement as they say their sound.

Whichever level you choose to work at, the groups need to present their performances to the rest of the group.

This may look simple, even silly. But it produces surprisingly striking effects. Students rapidly realize that they are capable of producing really impressive work. And that enhances motivation. It also helps shy or hesitant students get over their apprehension. They are shielded by the group and the fact that they are not singled out for attention. There is safety in numbers. Playing around with sounds, words, phrases like this helps students develop a physical feel for the language. This sense of the physicality of sounds – how it feels in the mouth – is an important way of relating to a new language.

These are activities to be done for a short time – but done often.

17 Drawing the Music

A recurring theme of this book is the value of incorporating artistic inputs and processes in our teaching. The main input here is music, which is a powerful stimulus for visualization and emotion. The activity below capitalizes on this by combining music, drawing, physical activity and language.

Before the activity you need to choose some excerpts of different kinds of music. For example, slow, gentle music like Erik Satie's *Gnossiennes*, fast, agitated music like parts of Stravinsky's *The Rite of Spring*, mood music like Debussy's *La Mer* or *Children's Corner*, lively but majestic music like Handel's *Water Music* or *Music for the Royal Fireworks*, graceful, rhythmical music like Tchaikovsky's *Swan Lake* or *The Nutcracker*, minimalist, repetitive music by composers like Philip Glass, Steve Reich or the intriguing work of Arvo Pärt, like *Spiegel im Spiegel*. Jazz is also good – John Coltrane, George Shearing or the MJQ for slower pieces, Dixieland or ragtime for more energetic pieces. But the choice is yours. The excerpts should not be too long however.

To prepare for the drawing activity, ask students to write the letters of the alphabet horizontally on a piece of paper individually or in pairs. They must then write an adjective beginning with each letter. For example, *anxious, boring, calm, deep, easy*, etc. Then play one of the musical excerpts. Which words in their list could fit the music? Repeat the activity with one or two more excerpts – choose ones as different from each other as possible. Ask if anyone 'saw' the music as it was played? What kinds of things did they visualize?

Explain that you are going to play three musical excerpts. Students need a large sheet of paper and a pen or marker. Tell them they should keep their eyes closed while the music is playing. As they listen they should move their pen across the paper in time with the way they feel the music is moving. Then play the three very short excerpts. Make sure they are very different. After this, let students compare the drawings they made. What words could describe the shapes they drew? For example, *jagged*, *round*, *sharp*, *smooth*, *spiky*, *wavy*, etc.

You can vary the activity by replacing the music with a text you read or play. Some texts which work well include: Noyes' *The Highwayman*, Auden's *Night Mail*, Tennyson's *The Charge of the Light Brigade*, the opening of Thomas' *Under Milk Wood*, etc. The main thing is to choose a text with a strong rhythm. Students again listen with eyes closed. They should focus on the sound of the text and not worry about understanding it – you can come back to that later.

Finally, play just one of the pieces of music. This time, students listen with eyes closed and let their visual imagination conjure up images. What do they 'see' with their mind's eye as the music plays? This time, play up to five minutes of music. Then ask them to draw some of the things they visualized. They do not need to make sophisticated pictures. But if anyone insists they cannot draw, let them write what they saw instead. They work in small groups sharing what they drew or wrote. Then make a display of their drawings and texts.

18 Writing Chants and Songs

The inventor of jazz chants was Carolyn Graham, who stumbled on the insight that the cadences of spoken colloquial (American) English perfectly matched the four-four rhythm of traditional jazz. Jazz chants offer scope for multiple but enjoyable repetition, and for intensive work on stress and rhythm.

What is so appealing about jazz chants is that they can be made up on the spot using naturally-occurring language, and that they provide massive repetition coupled with enjoyment. They also help students acquire the rhythmical heartbeat of the language.

At their simplest, jazz chants can be devised and used for enjoyable vocabulary practice. For example, you choose an area of lexis, say *clothing*, *food*, *fruit*, *health*, *vegetables*, etc. Students brainstorm three vocabulary items from the lexical area with one, two and three syllables respectively. They choose the items they want to use – a word with one syllable, one with two and one with three. You write these on the board in order of syllables: two, three, one. For example:

- *trousers, overcoats, shirts*
- *apples, oranges, grapes*
- *carrots, potatoes, leeks*
- *sunshine, thunderstorms, rain* (repeat twice)
- *sunshine, thunderstorms* (repeat twice)
- *sunshine, thunderstorms, rain* (just once)

Students then chant the chosen set of words, clapping to the rhythm, which gives a satisfying sound shape to the chant.

You can play around with ways of doing this, by allocating different words to different groups, by varying volume, speed, pitch, mood etc. You can also experiment with different syllable orders of words: *screwdrivers* (three), *hammers* (two), *nails* (one); *beef* (one), *chicken* (two), *sausages* (three); etc. You can add one four-syllable word or phrase as a final punchline. For example, *apples, oranges, grapes – avocados!*

Jazz chants can also be used to practise grammatical structures. You will need to decide on a pattern you want to practise. This should preferably have a strong rhythmical pattern. For example:

- Present simple for habitual actions: *Everybody talks but nobody listens.* This line would be repeated three times and followed by a punchline, such as, *It drives me mad.*
- Present progressive as future with know-type verbs: *I know where I'm meeting but I don't know the way.* This would also be spoken three times, then followed by a request – *Can you help me, please?* – spoken twice. The same pattern can be used with parallel sentences: *I know what I'm doing but I don't know what it's for. I know who I'm meeting but I don't know his room. I know how to get there but I don't know the price. I know what it's used for but I don't know how it works.* etc.

Any structure can be built into a chant like this. As students get used to using chants, they can be encouraged to develop their own. There is something almost addictive in using chants like these, and students can often be heard using them even outside class.

The third kind of chant involves making up short poems which can be recited as chants. Here is an example:

I've got those 6 o'clock blues
When they broadcast the news.
All it does is confuse
That's why I always refuse
To listen to the views
On the 6 o'clock news.
I've got those 6 o'clock blues.

These poems are relatively easy to write, especially if you use a stem as the basis. (See also **2 Growing Stems into Poems**.)

Graham, C. (2003) *Grammarchants: More Jazz Chants*. New York: Oxford University Press.

Graham, C. (2006) *Creating Chants and Songs*. Oxford: Oxford University Press.

New Songs for Old

> There is a long history of song tunes being hijacked
> and sung with new lyrics. Most school children know
> irreverent versions of Christmas carols, such as *When
> shepherds washed their socks by night...* . This activity
> aims to expose students to examples of parodies and to
> help them write parodies of their own.

You might start with some examples of simple parodies based on
children's rhymes. For example:

- *Mary had a little lamb. / Mary had a pot of jam.*
- *Twinkle, twinkle little star. / Barbie drove a little car.*

Then, let students listen to and sing along with a parody of a well-
known song, for example:

(To the tune of *She'll be Coming Round the Mountain When she Comes*):

She'll be
She'll be using her computer when she comes.
She'll be using her computer when she comes.
She'll be using her computer,
And no one could look cuter,
She'll be using her computer when she comes.

She'll be checking on her email when she comes.
She'll be checking on her email when she comes.
She'll be checking on her email,
She's an electronic female –
She'll be checking on her email when she comes.

She'll be sending SMSs when she comes.
She'll be sending SMSs when she comes.

She'll be sending SMSs,
While she's thinking of new dresses.
She'll be sending SMSs when she comes.

She'll be tweeting on her laptop when she comes.
She'll be tweeting on her laptop when she comes.
And nothing could be sweeter,
Than this laptop-packing tweeter,
She'll be tweeting on her laptop when she comes.

Tell students that they will be making a parody of a well-known song.
You can either suggest one or ask them to make suggestions. (If the
latter, they will need advance notice so that they can prepare suggestions
outside class.)

In order to write a parody, they first need to be thoroughly familiar
with the original, which means close attention to rhythm, rhyme and
repetition. Ask them to work in pairs and come up with a possible first
line of a parody based on *Frère Jacques*. For example, *Salt and pepper*
(repeated).

Write a number of the better examples on the board. Then ask the pairs
to choose one of the first lines and try to continue the parody, paying
attention to the verse structure and rhyming of the original. Pairs share
their first verse with the class. Let them sing it if they prefer. The final
version might look like this:

Salt and pepper (repeated)
On my fries (repeated)
Add a squeeze of lemon. (repeated)
Nice surprise. (repeated)

Ask students to write a second verse for homework. After discussion
and editing in the next class, ask them to make a class display of their
work. If they find the idea of parodies appealing, let them find more
examples and record these in a 'Parodies' file.

Human beings seem to be hard-wired for music, and especially for rhythm. And the rhythmic component of music is shared by language – every language has its signature rhythm. This activity encourages creative experimentation integrating music.

This activity is in two parts. In this first part, we begin by exploring the range of vocalizations and sounds which human beings can make to achieve musical effects. In the second part, we shall add the element of hands-on construction – students will make their own instruments before using them in performance. Clearly, this is not a one-lesson activity. It would best be presented as a project over a minimum of three lessons and perhaps more. As with most projects, at least some of the work is best done outside class.

Introduce the topic of music in a class discussion. Who likes music? What kinds of music do they like? Do they have favourite kinds of music, favourite artistes? What is the difference between music and noise? Discuss some of the elements of music: rhythm, tempo (speed), volume (loud, soft), melody (the tune), pitch (from high to low), single or multiple instruments/voices, texture (*staccato/legato*), etc.

Then discuss how humans can make music with their bodies. Elicit the different kinds of singing voice there are: soprano, mezzo-soprano, contralto, counter-tenor, tenor, baritone, bass. Ask students to demonstrate each voice-type by singing a line from a well-known song (e.g. *I've got plenty of nothing, and nothing's plenty for me* from *Porgy and Bess*). Point out that we also have a range of sounds which can be made with the hands (clapping, slapping) and the feet (stamping). Move on to the range of sounds the human voice can produce, for example, groaning, howling. In groups, ask students to list all these sounds, whether or not they have a meaning component. For example, throat clearing has no meaning, whereas tongue clicking (*ts-ts*) often indicates annoyance or disapproval. In feedback, students have to demonstrate the sound they are describing.

Here is a sample list – it is not comprehensive: *brrrr (lip flapping), burp, click, cough, gasp, giggle, groan, grunt, hum, laugh, lip popping, lip smacking, phew, shriek, sigh, sneeze, sniff, sob, squeal, suck in breath, trill, tut-tutting (ts-ts), ululation, whistle, yodel,* etc.

In groups of about six, students select a sound each, then work on an oral performance of their sounds, weaving them together into a kind of verbal collage (see **25 Performing Texts**). They then perform for the other groups.

In the same groups, they prepare an oral performance of this short poem:

> Cough, sniff, whistle, burp.
> Sigh, gasp, yodel, slurp.
> Click, sob, warble, sigh.
> Groan, click, gurgle … Why?
>
> Sounds that come both fast and slow,
> Sounds all chopped up, sounds that flow.
> Bass voice low, soprano high.
> Can anybody tell me – Why?

Afterwards, lead in to a discussion of the range of devices different languages use to make meaning. For example, the Bantu click languages, the use of pharyngeal and glottal sounds in Arabic, whistling languages in the Canary Islands, Mexico and New Guinea, nasal sounds in French, etc. Point out that what for us may be just a noise, in some languages may have meaning.

At first sight, this activity may seem to have little to do with learning English. However, it is valuable in a number of ways:

- it helps develop an awareness of the repertoire of sounds used in human languages.
- students can also become more aware of the organs of speech which produce sound.
- it is a physical activity, not simply asking students to sit and listen but to actively participate in the physical production of sounds.
- it opens up the whole, very rich lexical area of English vocabulary used for sounds.
- it is highly enjoyable, allowing students to make weird sounds in a framework of mutual support. It therefore helps to establish a cooperative learning atmosphere.

Improvising Musical Instruments: 2

Though this can be used as a free-standing activity, it is best used as a follow-on from 20. Here we move from the human voice to actual musical instruments.

Elicit from students what are the basic types of musical instruments. Essentially, all music results from striking a resonant surface (percussion), from vibrating a stretched string (strings) or blowing air through some kind of tube to make it resonate (wind). To introduce this in an entertaining way, show the Disney animated cartoon: *Toot, Whistle, Plunk and Boom*, Disney 1959. (https://www.youtube.com/watch?v=zjHrmmFIErY)

Divide students into groups of four. Each group then prepares a performance of this poem for the rest of the class (see **25 Performing Texts** for suggestions for doing this). Point out the strong rhythmic patterning in this poem.

> **The Orchestra Tuning Up**
> Plink, plonk, twiddle, thrum;
> Ping, pong, jingle, strum;
> Clink, chink, rattle, hum;
> Clank, twang, tinkle, drum.
>
> Tick, tock, clatter, bong;
> Chime, clash, jangle, gong;
> Swish, blare, whistle, clang;
> Peep, boing, ding-dong, bang.
>
> Tootle, rumble, batter, plop;
> Pom-pom, tiddle-tiddle, pom-pom …
> STOP!

Ask students for ideas about how to use common, everyday objects to improvise musical instruments. Explain that there is a very wide range of quite sophisticated instruments which can be devised from readily available materials. Then show them the YouTube of Favio Chavez, in Cateura, Paraguay which shows a complete orchestra of instruments improvised from scrap. (https://www.youtube.com/watch?v=yiYFcuIkBjU)

Explain that the class project will be to improvise a range of instruments which will then be used in a performance. The class will also prepare a report on how they carried out the project, with photographs and, if possible, a video of what they did. Set a time limit, say a week, for students to bring their instruments to class. There are many web-links offering useful ideas.

When students bring in their instruments, check that they work, and let them try out how they might work together, with special emphasis on rhythm. The music will accompany a text in some way so it is better to use a relatively short text with a strong rhythm. This is an example of the kind of text which might be used:

People
Some people speak.
Some people are shy.
Some people laugh.
Some people cry.

Some people come early.
Some people come late.
Some people are boring.
Some people are great!

Some people are honest.
Some people lie.
Some people live.
Some people die.

Allow plenty of time for groups to discuss how they will merge the words and the music. They will need to rehearse outside class. If possible, video the performances. Following the public performance, organise the writing and printing of their reports.

22 Moved by Music

Music implies movement, and it is hard for humans to resist moving in time with a musical beat. The rhythms of music are also closely related to those of language. So the combination of music, movement and language seems like a perfect marriage for language teaching.

If you do decide to work with music and movement, you need an open space where students can move freely. You may be able to clear a space in your classroom but it is even better if you can move into a hall or gym for this kind of work. Students also need to be wearing loose and comfortable clothing, and to remove their shoes.

You may want to explain why they will be working with music and movement. Tell them about the cognitive/learning benefits of both music and movement. Explain that music and language share many features, not least rhythm. Answer any questions or objections.

There is a vast range of choice for pieces suitable for movement. Every teacher will have their own preferences, and over time will discover by trial and error, which pieces work best. Here are just a few suggestions to get started: Milhaud *Le Boeuf sur le Toit*, Saint-Saëns *The Carnival of the Animals*, Satie *Gymnopédies*, Ravel *La Valse*, Smetana *Má vlast*, Stravinsky *The Rite of Spring*, Grieg *The Holberg Suite*, Elgar *The Serenade for Strings*, Barber *Adagio for Strings*, Beethoven 6th *Symphony*. You might also want to try *Bossa Nova, Salsa, Tango*, or other dance rhythms, though it is best to avoid lyrics. *Klezmer* music can also work well.

Here are some brief suggestions for activities:

- Free movement. Students move to the music any way they choose. When you stop the music, they freeze. Re-start the music. When it stops, they must work with the person nearest them, and try to mirror each other's movements.

- Directed movement. As students move, give instructions: *go higher, go lower, curl up small, spread out, you are heavier/lighter, move faster/slower, move more smoothly/more agitatedly*, etc. *Now show your feelings in the way you move: happiness, sadness, disappointment, anger, confusion, excitement, shame, pride, disgust*, etc. (This is a kind of modified Total Physical Response. It also links with the work of the influential choreographer, Rudolf Laban.)
- Give students cards with nouns on them: *a fish, a flower opening, an eagle, a heron, an antelope, an elephant, a tree in the wind, a dog looking for a bone*, etc. They move to convey what is on their card.
- Prepare cards with a word on them, one per student. All the words form a semantic network. For example: *time – ages, early, good, hard, late, long, passing, short, spent, wasted*, etc. Students speak their words as they move to the music. You can also use phrases, proverbs or quotations. Students move to the music and speak their lines. Signal that they should come together in a tableau just before the music ends. They stand in silence for a moment after the music stops, then start to speak their words or lines as an overlapping vocal mosaic or tapestry. Stop them after about three minutes.

Make sure there is a video or photographic record of students' work for feedback discussion and display to other groups.

http://helgesenhandouts.weebly.com/energy-breaks1.html

Newlove, J. (2003) *Laban for All*. London: Nick Hern Books.

Ratey, J. J. and Hagerman, E. (2010) *Spark: How exercise will improve the performance of your brain*. London: Quercus.

Sousa, D. A. (2011) *How the Brain Learns*. Thousand Oaks, CA: Corwin.

Words and Music

Words and music seem to enjoy each other's company. The most common way of harnessing this to ELT has been through using songs in class. However, this activity presents a more demanding way of working with words and music. It is a project which can extend over a whole term or course.

Introduce the idea of working with words and music by referring to some well-known examples of texts (and sometimes film, too) accompanied by music. Some good examples would be: Prokofiev's *Peter and the Wolf*, Poulenc's *The Story of Babar*, Auden and Britten's *Night Mail* and their O *Tell me the Truth about Love*, Dylan Thomas' *Under Milk Wood* with Stan Tracey's *Jazz Suite*. These are available online and it would be ideal if you can show at least one of them as part of the introduction. Draw students' attention to the way the text and the music are woven together.

Explain that this will be a group project to produce a recording or live performance by a specific deadline, plus a presentation to explain the performance. In some cases students will work with existing text plus music, in others with text for which they must find or create the music, in others with music for which they will create the words. Students will work in groups of three or four. Much of their work will be done outside class, with regular short feedback and monitoring sessions in class.

Their first task will be to choose which project they will work on. Here are some suggestions:

- *The Snowman* by Raymond Briggs. This is readily available. It is an animated cartoon film, which has a musical accompaniment but no speech. The task will be to write the story, then record the voice-over to fit the visual and musical story. Students will need to become thoroughly familiar with the story and fit their text in at appropriate points.

- Using the *I Have a Dream* speech by Martin Luther King, the group will have to find (or compose) music as an accompaniment. This will involve fine judgements about pace, pausing, volume and so on so that the music fits the text as neatly as possible. There are, of course, plenty of other texts they might use: extracts from Noyes' *The Highwayman*, sections of Penelope Shuttle's *Redgrove's Wife*, *Funeral Blues* (*Stop all the clocks...*) by Auden, made famous in the film *Four Weddings and a Funeral*. You will know best which texts are appropriate as to level, and more likely to appeal to your class.
- Finding a piece of music, then looking for a text which will fit it. For example, what kind of text might fit a Chopin Mazurka or Nocturne, or *Finlandia* by Sibelius? This would involve them in extensive searches for texts. Good selections are available in *The Rattlebag* (Faber & Faber), *The Nation's Favourite Poems* (Penguin), *Poems that Make Grown Men Cry* (Simon & Schuster), and the many other anthologies of poetry.
- Writing a poem or text and setting it to music they have composed. Here students might write or re-use as their text a stem poem (see **2 Growing Stems into Poems**) such as *If you were a ... you'd be ...* . There will almost certainly be students who play a musical instrument or who are familiar with synthesizers. They might also use some of the improvised musical instruments from activities **20** and **21**.

Once students have selected their project, brief them on how to go about it. They should draw up a schedule, setting deadlines for finishing various aspects of the project. They then need to decide on who will carry out which roles: text researcher, musical director, rehearsal manager etc. Make sure they write this down. Then build in regular monitoring sessions for each group with you. Make sure they leave adequate time for sound and/or video recordings.

Set a time and date for a performance in which groups will present orally, in English, something about their project, then show or play their work.

C: Working with Drama and the Voice

This section offers a range of activities which draw on theatre training skills. Many involve improvisation, oral expressivity and movement.

Sculpting a Tableau

This activity involves a lot of body movement but also calls upon students to visualize, which as we have seen can enhance learning. It also involves close observation and visual recall, and many opportunities for interactive discussion.

Explain to students what a living tableau is: a kind of sculpture made up of the bodies of the participants. Students then need to work in groups – the group size will depend on the number of characters needed for the tableau.

You can use a number of stimuli for forming a tableau. The most obvious is to give each group a picture containing a number of people. Beryl Cook's lively paintings are a rich source. But the world of art is full of good material: Rembrandt's *The Nightwatch* (largish group), Manet's *Le Déjeuner sur l'herbe* (only four characters), Seurat's *Bathers at Asnières*, Renoir's *Bal du moulin de la Galette*. Photographs can also be used.

An alternative stimulus is to use a description from a story. This adds an additional interpretative layer, as students need first to translate words into visualization. Here is a brief example:

> I remembered the last time I'd seen her. She was sitting at the breakfast table, a letter in her hand and tears in her eyes. Her sister stood behind her looking down with her hand resting on her shoulder and her mother was facing her across the table, holding the teapot, ready to pour. In the doorway, her father stood holding her son's hand, preventing him from running towards her. The atmosphere was thick with grief.

Before groups start, they need to discuss the allocation of characters. Assign one student the role of class photographer (or video manager), whose job it is to make a photographic record or video of the finished tableaux and of some of the preparation stages. This will also involve giving instructions to the others. Photographs of the tableaux can then be combined with texts the groups write later to become a catalogue of the 'exhibition'.

The organizer gives directions to the rest of the group to form a tableau that resembles the picture or textual description as closely as possible. Clearly there will be lots of vocabulary associated with the human body, and locational language describing where items are in relation to each other. It is better to set a time limit of about 15 minutes for this stage.

Groups dissolve their tableaux. They work together to give it a title, then write a brief text which would appear next to the photograph of the tableaux in an exhibition.

Groups then take it in turn to present their tableau to the other groups. Before they do so, one of them reads aloud the short descriptive text they have written. The other groups observe and comment on the accuracy of the representation.

If there is time, each group works with one other group. Group A observes Group B's tableau. They then have to replicate it as accurately as possible. Group B members can give comments and instructions. Then Group B observes Group A's tableau and repeats the process.

Ratey, J. J. and Hagerman, E. (2010) *Spark: How exercise will improve the performance of your brain*. London: Quercus.

Tomlinson, B. (2011) 'Seeing what they mean: helping L2 readers to visualize.' In Tomlinson, B. (ed.) *Materials Development in Language Teaching*. Cambridge: Cambridge University Press.

Performing Texts

> To learn a language, we need to experience it in multiple repetitions but repetition can be very monotonous and demotivating. However, we can devise activities where repetition occurs naturally. Performing texts is one enjoyable way of doing this.

This activity is based on the idea of *Readers' Theater* developed by Courtney Cazden and others in the US, though in its original form, Readers' Theater tends to develop scripts from prose texts (including non-literary texts) which are then performed. Many claim that Readers' Theater helps slow readers as well as improving oral fluency. This is an activity which, in my experience, has never failed to engage students in the cooperative achievement of the performance. Done regularly, it works wonders for student motivation, self-confidence and expressive ability.

Choose a text which lends itself to performance (see the example below). Make sure it is not too long. Explain to students that they will be performing the text as an ensemble, where everyone has to participate. The aim is to make the text as interesting to listen to as possible.

Chickens
There are chickens in the garden.
There are chickens on the stairs.
Chickens next to Dad's armchair.
Chickens everywhere.

Chickens inside cupboards,
Chickens down the street,
Chickens under tables,
Chickens round my feet.

There are chickens in the deep freeze,
Chickens in the soup,
Chickens among the bedsheets,
Chickens in the coop.

There are chickens in the flowerbeds,
Chickens all over the car,
Chickens all around the house –
And even in the bar!

Before students start, remind them of ways they can vary their voices by playing with volume, pitch level and range, pace and pausing, intensity and energy, voice quality and manner and modulation showing mood and tone.

Suggest that they think about: variety, energy, clarity (the audience needs to hear clearly), interpretation (is this to be humorous, moving, angry, etc.?), possible movement, sound effects or background music, how many people speak at once (which parts will need a single speaker, several speakers, everyone, etc.?).

Students work in groups of about five to six. Allow them at least 20 minutes to read and discuss how they will perform the text. They then rehearse it. Depending on the length of the class, it is sometimes better if they rehearse outside class and perform in the next class.

When they perform, make sure they stand up and face the audience. There is usually a lot of excitement so remind them to listen to other groups, if they want other groups to listen to them! After everyone has performed, hold a discussion about their impressions of their experience.

There are psychological and pedagogical advantages to this activity. Students have the text, so they can be secure in what they have to say. Peripheral language learning takes place as they focus on performance. Performance is enjoyable and motivating and generates high levels of engagement and excitement. It also encourages play and experimentation. The activity fosters interactive discussion and helps build group solidarity. Repetition is painless yet leads to memorization, which in turn can lead to subconscious acquisition. Physical activity is combined with both cognitive and affective engagement. It involves indirect pronunciation work, especially on suprasegmental features like stress and intonation. Because of the high level of involvement, texts are processed in greater depth: students' understanding is enhanced from the inside, rather than externally through comprehension questions.

Actors in rehearsal are encouraged to play around with their lines. By 'stretching' the text, they become familiar with it, so that when they read it 'normally' their voice is usually more interesting. We can do the same with our students – engaging in lots of repetition without the usual boredom.

First, select a short text, either prose or poetry. Here is an example:

> You are my black; you are my white.
> You are my darkness and my light.
> You are my blindness and my sight.
> You are my day; you are my night.

Students work in groups of four. Each student reads a line in turn.

Student one reads very slowly, student two reads as fast as possible, student three reads very softly, student four reads very loudly, student one reads in a happy voice, student two reads in a sad voice, student three reads in an angry voice, student four reads in a romantic voice, etc.

They then do the activity again, but student one starts by reading very fast, student two reads very softly, student three reads very loudly, and so on, so that everyone reads in a different way from the first round. They continue the activity until everyone has read in every way or until they are exhausted!

In a later class, repeat the activity but with other variations in modes of speaking. For example:

- Reading in a very high or very low pitch.
- Reading each line with a different intonation pattern (flat, from low to high, from high to low, etc.).
- Changing the stress in each line.
- Reading each line around the group, each student speaking one word in turn, keeping the natural rhythm as far as possible.

- Reading the first word aloud and mouthing the other words silently.
- Mouthing the words silently until the last word, which is read aloud.
- Speaking the lines using only the vowel sounds of the words.
- Speaking the lines using only the consonant sounds of the words.

Finally, each student reads the whole text in a 'normal' way.

A further variation is to ask students to accompany their reading of the line with a movement.

To extend this activity, choose another short and simple text. For example:

> The strange girl led him through a steel door into a dark cave. Suddenly the door slammed behind them. It was locked. 'We're trapped. There's no way out,' said the man. 'Not "we", just you,' said the girl, and she walked through the solid steel door and disappeared forever.

Students work in pairs. First they play around with the text using the ideas above. They then perform the text for another pair, reading alternate sentences with full expression.

The main point of this activity is to work on verbal fluency and pronunciation and to show how small variations in the way we say things can make a big difference to how people understand them. It also strengthens students' self-confidence, mutual trust and cooperation.

Linklater, K. (1992) *Freeing the Natural Voice*. New York: Theatre Communications Group.

Maley, A. (2000) *The Language Teacher's Voice*. London: Macmillan.

Martin, S. and Darnley, L. (2004) *The Teaching Voice*. New Jersey: Wiley.

McCallion, M. (1988) *The Voice Book: For Actors, Public Speakers and Everyone Who Want to Make the Most of Their Voice*. London: Faber & Faber.

Rodenburg, P. (1998) *The Actor Speaks*. London: Methuen.

> Most people have the capacity to make mental representations of what they read or hear in language. And visualization has been shown to enhance learning.

In this activity, students are asked to use visualization to generate language. There are at least two ways of doing this:

- Expanding a story through questions and visualization. You need to find a shortish story with plenty of visual elements. See the example below. You read the story sentence by sentence. At the end of each sentence, ask students to close their eyes and try to imagine the scene. You then ask questions to elicit more detailed information. For example: *There was a young man who was unlucky and a failure.* Questions might be: *What is he wearing? How tall is he? Is he thin or fat? What does his hair look like? Is he carrying anything? Can you see the expression on his face? Where is he standing now? Why was he unlucky? What happened to make him a failure?* etc. By the end of the story, students will have a much richer understanding of it and will have had plenty of language practice.
- Visualizing a place or character chosen by the student. Tell the story from beginning to end. Then ask individual students to retell it, while others correct or expand on what the individual student is saying. When students are familiar with the story, ask them to choose just one episode in it. They should imagine themselves at that point in the story. What can they observe? To help them with more detailed visualization, use the five senses and the seven questions – *what, where, when, why, who, how* and *Is/Are…?* Students should write down their answers. They work in pairs exchanging their descriptions, then each writes a short piece – poem or description – of what they visualized.

There was a young man who was unlucky and a failure. He hears about the Master of Luck at the end of the world and sets off to find him. He trips over a bag of bones in the road –it is a starving wolf. The wolf begs him to ask the Master of Luck what he should do. He goes on and comes to a tree. It is dying and looks dry and leafless. The tree also begs him to ask the Master of Luck what it should do. He goes on and comes to a big house. A beautiful young girl is crying because she is unhappy. She too begs him to ask the Master of Luck what she should do. He finds the Master of Luck and asks what the young woman, the tree and the wolf should do. The Master tells him: The young woman is unhappy because she needs a husband to love her. She will make him very happy. The tree is withered because there is a box full of gold trapped in its roots. When someone digs up the gold, it will grow well again. The wolf is hungry. It should eat the first fool who comes along, then it will be strong again. 'And what about me? How will I find my luck?' he asks. The Master tells him, 'Your luck is waiting for you – right there in front of you. All you have to do is see it.' The young man goes back the way he came. He tells the young woman, 'You need to get married to a nice young man.' 'Then please marry me,' she says. 'Sorry. I don't have time. I must get home and find my luck.' He tells the tree about the gold. 'Then please dig it up,' says the tree. 'Sorry, I don't have time. I need to get home to find my luck.' He comes to the wolf, and tells him what the Master said. So the wolf eats him!

Impro is short for Improvisation. Participants do not know what will happen next in an interaction and must react in the moment. By doing Impro work regularly, we can help our students become 'comfortable with being uncomfortable', and enhance their ability to deal with the unexpected.

Impro is not one activity but many, so here are just a couple of ideas for working with Impro in your classroom. First, here are two possible warm-ups:

- Students face each other in pairs. They each place a coin on their right palm, which they hold out at chest level. The game is to carry on a simple conversation (you can suggest a topic) while trying to distract their partner and to snatch their coin from them. It is important to keep talking.
- Students work in groups of about eight. The aim is to count to ten. But each number must be called by just one student at a time. Anyone in the group can speak, but they are not allowed to go round the circle sequentially. If two students speak at once, they go back to one. No signals or gestures are allowed. The group just has to find a way of speaking the ten numbers without any overlapping.

And these are more extended Impro activities:

- Story with interruptions. Ask students to prepare a short story to tell the class. They should also think of an unrelated content word. Students should not reveal their stories or words to the rest of the class. Nominate the first storyteller and five students to contribute their words. Explain that the storyteller will tell their story and the other five students will call out their words one at a time during the story. The storyteller must incorporate the word into their story. For example: *A funny thing happened on my way to town on*

Saturday. I caught the bus and it was full as usual. (Random word one: *dandruff.*) *I had to stand next to an old man who had lots of dandruff. It was like a snowstorm on his shoulders. Anyway, when the bus got to the terminus I noticed this girl getting off.* (Random word two: *hasty.*) *I thought she looked really nice but I didn't want to be too hasty so...* etc. Let several students have turns at being the storyteller and make sure everyone has the chance to put in a random word at some point.

- Improvising a scene using objects. Students can work in pairs or threes. It will help if they each wear a red nose and a different hat. Clear an acting space. One student clown comes on and explores the space. The second comes on and they continue to explore the space together, noticing things – either silently or with dialogue. Add a cardboard box to the space. They react to this new item. Later, add another object – perhaps an apple, an umbrella, a mobile phone ... . Students go on exploring and gradually developing a storyline. Throughout, they need to stay in eye contact with the audience (the rest of the class).

Make sure there is detailed discussion about what happened and questions to the clowns: what the story was, why the clowns performed certain actions, etc. This is where the language work comes in. To facilitate feedback, try to ensure that sessions are videoed. The videos can also be made available on the class or school website.

Johnstone, K. (1999) *Impro for storytellers: Theatresports and the Art of Making Things Happen.* London: Faber & Faber.

Johnstone, K. (2007) *Impro: Improvisation and the Theatre.* London: Methuen.

Poynton, R. (2013) *DO/IMPROVISE.* London: The Do Books Co.

> Withholding information makes us more eager to know what is being withheld. It also increases our sensitivity to any clues as to what the solution might be.

The activity below is based on mime – conveying information through the use of the body without using words. It is in fact a version of the party game, *Charades*, adapted for language learning purposes. Essentially, one person has some information and tries to convey that to others through mime and gesture. It is a lot of fun but it also involves the repeated and in-depth use of language, drawing on everyone's linguistic data bank.

You will need to prepare slips of paper before class with messages for the guests to use. The messages should be worded roughly at the proficiency level of the class. They can be linked to structures currently being studied more formally. Here are some possible messages:

- *Can someone please help me with my suitcases?*
- *There's a snake in my toilet. Please send someone at once.*
- *Can you tell me the way to the nearest Post Office?*
- *How much does it cost to send a postcard to China by airmail?*
- *I just tried to get into my room but there are two small dogs in the bed.*
- *I turned the tap on in the bath and now I can't turn it off. Please help!*
- *There's something wrong with my bill. I have a special discount but you have charged me the whole amount.*

You need to set up the classroom specially for this activity. At the front of the class, put a chair in front of a table and leave space for someone to stand on the other side of the table, facing the classroom. This represents the reception desk in the hotel lobby. One student will be the hotel receptionist with their back to the room. Another student will be a hotel guest. You will give each hotel guest a slip of paper with the message on it just before the game starts. Only the guest can see this and must not show it to anyone else.

The rest of the class should form a semi-circle facing the table so that they have a clear view.

Explain that the guest has a physical condition which prevents them from speaking: they can only communicate through gesture. The hotel receptionist has to try to understand the message and offer possible interpretations verbally, which the guest can respond to non-verbally, perhaps by nodding or shaking the head. Anyone in the class can also offer interpretations. When a correct solution is arrived at, the person who found it will be the next in turn to be the guest, with a new slip of paper.

Tell the class that there are two distinct stages for the game. The first is to guess the general content of the message. For example: *You are looking for the post office.* The second stage is finding the precise wording of the message on the slip of paper: *Can you tell me the way to the nearest Post Office?*

The second stage is very important. The need to find the precise wording of the message is key to the activity. It forces students to trawl through all their linguistic resources, trying out multiple permutations until they hit on the correct one. The fact that everyone can contribute involves them in sharing whatever they can. And even those who are not speaking are sub-vocally trying things out and listening to what the others are saying.

This is not a new activity but I make no apology for that. It is one of the near-fail-safe activities in my repertoire. It is hard to beat for the level of in-depth engagement it generates.

This activity is to help students learn some of the skills needed to become an effective storyteller or raconteur, thus gaining self-confidence and oral fluency.

Introduce the topic by asking students if they like stories and jokes and if they can tell a story or joke in English. Allow time for this, perhaps by giving a few minutes for pair work where students recall some stories or jokes. The class listens to one or two of them.

Students first discuss these questions in small groups:

- *How do we choose the story or joke?*
- *Will it interest the audience?*
- *Will it offend anyone?* (Especially important for jokes.)
- *Is it about the right length?*
- *How will we remember it?*
- *Is it important to speak in character?*
- *Will we need any props, like pictures or objects to illustrate points?*

Then offer students this advice:

- It is better not to try to learn the words by heart but to learn the story line. One way of doing this is to make a story skeleton (see below), which has the main elements in note form. Rehearse the story with a friend and get feedback.
- Try telling it in different ways, varying speed, pausing, volume, voice quality.

Then ask students in small groups to discuss how to perform a story or joke, using these questions:

- *How will we establish rapport with our listeners?*
- *How will we hold their interest?*

Then offer this advice:

- You can establish rapport by asking leading questions before you start. For example, for Gellert (see below): *Does anyone have a pet dog? Are dogs dangerous? What about wolves? Has anyone seen a wolf? Have you heard the proverb: Act in haste: repent at leisure? What do you think it means?*

- Address everyone in the room, not just those in front of you. Establish eye contact. Smile. Continue to ask questions: *So what do you think he did next? What would you have done?* etc.
- Repeat things in slightly different ways to give them time to process information: *He couldn't find his son. His son was nowhere to be found. He looked everywhere for his son but couldn't find him.*
- Make sure your voice is clear and audible to everyone. Don't speak too fast. Use pauses for effect. Don't go on for too long.

Ask half the students to choose and prepare a story – the other half, a joke. They will perform it in a later class. Bring in a 'magic story stick', which they will pass to each player to show they have become Storyteller. Students will evaluate their classmates' preparation and performance skills.

Story skeleton for Gellert
Man has baby son and faithful dog (Gellert). Goes hunting and leaves son with dog. Wolves attack the house. Dog kills one and chases away the rest. Man returns and finds blood everywhere. Can't find his son. Thinks Gellert has killed him. Kills Gellert. Then finds son in the barn sitting by dead wolf. Too late.

Joke skeleton
Up in aeroplane. 3 people: schoolgirl, priest, the President. Plane starts to crash. Only 2 parachutes. President grabs one and jumps out. Priest tells girl, 'Take the other one. I will go to heaven instead.' Girl says: 'No need. The President grabbed my school rucksack.'

Heathfield, D. (2014) *Storytelling with our Students*. London: Delta.

Medgyes, P. (2002) *Laughing Matters: Humour in the Language Classroom*. Cambridge: Cambridge University Press.

Morgan, J. and Rinvolucri, M. (1984) *Once Upon a Time: Using Stories in the Language Classroom*. Cambridge: Cambridge University Press.

Taylor, E. K. (2000) *Using Folktales*. Cambridge: Cambridge University Press.

Wajnryb, R. (2003) *Stories*. Cambridge: Cambridge University Press.

Wright, A. (2009) *Storytelling with Children*. Oxford: Oxford University Press.

Making Masks

> Many students are self-conscious when learning another language. Using a mask largely removes the fear of 'losing face' by allowing the wearers to adopt another 'face' and temporarily to forget themselves by becoming someone else.

There is a large variety of mask types, ranging from full-face, to half-face to eyes-only; and from blank, featureless masks to stereotypical character masks as in the Commedia dell'Arte. And they are likewise made of a wide variety of materials – including leather, wood, latex and paper. They are relatively easy to buy, and some teachers like to have a set of commercially available masks. However, simple masks are easy to make and students enjoy making them as part of a masks project. This also gives them ownership of their mask and helps create a sense of shared achievement.

The simplest form of mask can be made from large, disposable, paper dinner plates. Students have one each, scissors and some thin string. Using their finger and thumb spread they measure the distance between their eyes, and transfer this to the paper plate and mark it. They then cut out the eye holes. Cutting out the mouth is optional. They make small holes for the string (or elastic) which can then be tied to keep the mask in place. Alternatively, they can cut the shape of the mask from large sheets of manila or other stiff paper. This is good for making half-masks. If you decide to have character masks, students then decorate the face accordingly using coloured markers.

In using them, remember that masks carry a mysterious aura and should be treated accordingly. Students should never be seen putting on their masks. This can be the first exercise, done without speaking. Ask students to go outside the door, then come back into the room wearing their mask. Tell them to decide:

- Who are you when you come in?
- How will you stand, walk, look at the audience?

Take time for this so that students start to feel the effect of the mask. Conduct a feedback session where they can comment on how they felt and what they noticed about classmates' performances.

Follow up by asking students, wearing their masks, to imagine that they have a string attached to a part of their body, and someone is gently pulling them in a particular direction. Vary the part of the body the string is attached to.

Call out an emotion (e.g. *hope, frustration, admiration*, etc.). Wearing their masks, students convey the emotion. Neutral masks are better for this.

Students work in small groups. Each group acts out an emotion (e.g *anger, disappointment, grief*, etc.). The rest of the class has to guess what it is.

Give students scenarios to develop in pairs. For example, tell Student A they are having difficulties with an umbrella, a zip, threading a needle, opening a can, finding keys, etc. Tell them that if anyone tries to help they must refuse. Student B is told they must insist on helping. A starts the performance, then B joins them and offers to help. While they are acting, put a cardboard box in the corner. What will they do? Trust the process; something will happen.

Because these activities are largely done without words the importance of the feedback discussion is crucial. Also, make sure all these activities are videoed so that there is a class record of students' work.

If you do mask work, do it regularly so that students improve. Ideas you could not anticipate will come from them.

> **Puppets of different kinds are almost universal in human culture. They have long provided entertainment and common-sense lessons in life. And they continue to exercise a fascination not only for children but for adults too.**

Using puppets for language teaching can spark creativity in various ways. Students can make their own puppets, thus combining opportunities for using language with physical activity, and for using their imagination to create characters. This gives them real ownership of the puppets they will then use to dramatize dialogues, skits and stories. The scripts for performance can also be written by the students themselves as part of a writing activity.

The activities described here would need to be done over a number of lessons, and could be incorporated in your repertoire for regular use throughout a course.

There is one way of making a simple glove puppet at the end of the activity. Students work alone or in pairs and use the work card below.

Depending on your tolerance of mess, you can also provide papier mâché which students can use to sculpt the puppet's features. There are websites which show how to make papier mâché.

When all the puppets are ready, students mingle and the puppets introduce themselves to each other. You can either leave this to their imagination or provide guidelines: *Hello. I am* (name). *I live in* (place). *I am a* (occupation or character). *What is your name?* etc. Then have a feedback session where all the puppets are displayed and introduced.

You can work with the students to make a proper puppet theatre, but this is not necessary. The puppeteers can sit behind a table turned on its side, or you can use a big cardboard carton turned on its side with the bottom surface removed so the puppets can be moved from below. You can find more ideas on many aspects of making and using puppets by checking websites.

Your Glove Puppet

1. You will need: an old newspaper, some adhesive tape, some glue or paste, about 12 strips of white paper (2 cm × 12 cm), some paints, some pieces of cloth from old clothes (about 25 cm × 25 cm) and scissors.

2. Roll your newspaper into a long tube and secure it with adhesive tape so that it does not unroll.

3. Roll one end of the tube downward so that it forms an oval shape. Secure it with adhesive tape. This will be your puppet's head.

4. Using glue or paste, stick the strips of paper all over the head so that it has a smooth white surface. Leave it for a day to dry.

5. The next day, use the paints to draw the puppet's face. Decide what kind of person (or animal) it will be. You may want to add hair too. (Shredded paper or knitting wool is good for this.)

6. You now have a head on a long neck (the tube). You need to cut the neck so that it is just long enough for your first finger.

7. Tie or sew the piece of cloth around the puppet's neck to form its clothing.

8. Put your finger under the clothes and into the hole in the tube. Say 'Hello' to your puppet and give it a name. Where does it live? What kind of a character is it?

Aim to build up a whole cast of puppets over time, both general-purpose puppets: women, children etc., specific characters: doctor, soldier etc., and animals: dog, monkey etc. Students will usually invest a lot of creative effort in making these character puppets and can recycle language as they do so. This store of characters can then be used for a variety of purposes.

The puppet theatre can become the focus for acting out different kinds of text, depending on the level and interests of the students. These would include:

- Simple dialogues. These can be drawn from the coursebook in use. It may come as a surprise that even quite humdrum dialogues can be transformed when imaginatively projected through the puppets. Students can also write their own mini-dialogues based on everyday exchanges of greetings, requests, enquiries, etc. For example:

  A: *Excuse me. I am lost. Can you tell me the way to the (library, supermarket, police station, etc.)?*
  B: *Of course, no problem. Just go straight for about 300 metres, then turn right and it's just in front of you.* (Directions can be varied in different performances.)
  A: *So, straight on, then right?*
  B: *That's correct.*
  A: *Thanks so much.*
  B: *No problem.*

- Short sketches telling a story. There are many readily available stories which you or your students can easily adapt as pieces for performance. Apart from the Western fairy stories based on Grimms' tales and La Fontaine's fables, there are the Nasruddin stories from the Middle East, the Panchatantra from India, the Ananse stories from West Africa (and their Brer Rabbit versions in the American

South) – these can all be easily accessed on websites. (See also the storytelling books referred to in **30 Telling Jokes and Stories**.)

There is a story skeleton of an Ananse story below which could be adapted as a puppet play.

- Longer playlets or scenes from novels, stories and plays. With more advanced students, groups can work on prose texts or scenes from plays to adapt them for the puppet theatre.

Once texts are agreed, students can work in groups with the same number of characters as the text. They need to agree on allocation of characters, on the puppets they will use (they may need to make some extra ones), and on how they will stage the play – will they make a cardboard box theatre or use a table on its side? Characters will need to learn their words (at home), then rehearse how they will speak the lines, how characters will move, etc. Encourage students to film the performances. These can then be edited into a film with titles, captions etc.

Using puppets helps even shy students to gain confidence from being out of sight. Also, using their bodies (hands) appeals to many students. Imaginatively projecting a character is also motivating.

Ananse story skeleton

Characters: Ananse, his wife, his son, Father Thunder, a neighbour. Props: a pot, a stick.

Ananse and Father Thunder: Ananse very hungry – sees island with coconut trees – paddles there in canoe – drops coconut in the sea – falls on Father Thunder's house under the sea – Ananse goes down under sea – tells Father Thunder he is starving – Father T gives him a magic pot – when you are hungry, tell the pot 'Do as Father T says' – Ananse goes back to shore – tells pot 'Do what Father T says' – pot starts to produce delicious food – Ananse is greedy – hides the pot from wife and son – but son sees Ananse using pot and tells mother – mother angry – tells all neighbours to come – tells pot 'Do as Father T says' – food for everyone but then the pot explodes from over-use – Ananse angry but goes back to see Father T under sea – this time Father T gives him a stick – when he tells stick 'Do what Father T says', the stick beats him without stopping.

D: Playing with Language

The activities in this section encourage learners to take risks with the language by engaging with it in playful and enjoyable ways.

34 Doing the Opposite

> We are all creatures of habit: developing habitual routines
> saves time. But unless you break a habit, you will never
> find out how things might change without it. Here are a
> few ways you might consider reversing 'normal' habits.

Left-hand dictation is one example of breaking with a habit. It usually
leads to some very animated discussion at the end. Select a very short
text for dictation. Here is an example:

> 'I've never felt finer,'
> said the Queen of China,
> sitting down to dinner,
> 'But if I eat as much as this every day,
> I shall never get any thinner.'

Tell the class you will be giving a dictation but everyone will have to
write using their non-dominant hand. (If students are right-handed, they
will write with the left, and vice versa.) Then give the dictation. First
read it twice at normal speed so students get an idea of what it is about.
Then read it in shorter chunks, with pauses for them to write. At the
end, read it once more at normal speed. Then students exchange their
versions. Finally, give students the actual text.

In discussion, ask students about what happened, what they felt, what they
found most difficult. Was it more or less difficult to focus on the meaning
while they were struggling with the unfamiliar hand? What did they notice?

Alternative ways to break the pattern of dictations would be to ask
students:

- to write with their eyes closed
- to write standing up (or lying down if this is feasible)
- to write while a message about something different is played
- to draw the meaning of the text rather than writing it
- to write down only the six most important words in the text.

In *reverse dictation*, select a short text for dictation. Read it to the class twice from beginning to end, so they have a rough idea of what it is about. Then you dictate it, without stopping, from the end to the beginning. You then dictate it in short chunks starting from the end. Encourage students to discuss what they just did. Was it more difficult? More interesting? What did they notice about how they did it?

For *reverse reading* prepare a short text written out in reverse order. Here is an example:

emit dna edit tiaw rof on nam

Then allow just five minutes for students to re-constitute the text. Again, encourage them to talk about their experience. What effect did it have on their level of concentration? How quickly were they able to predict a word?

Normally, when we give a dictation, the students write it down immediately. In this activity, we reverse this process: they hear it, memorize it, and write it down later. Choose a short but compelling text for *memory dictation*. Here is an example:

> Nasruddin was walking round his house dropping breadcrumbs. His neighbour asked him, 'Why are you doing that?' 'It's to keep the tigers away,' replied Nasruddin. 'But there aren't any tigers around here,' said his neighbour. 'That's right. So this is very effective, isn't it?' replied Nasruddin, triumphantly.

First read the text twice at slow, normal speed. Then discuss what it might mean. Then read it one more time. The next lesson, ask students to write out the story from memory. If it helps, write up some prompts: *breadcrumbs … neighbour … tigers … effective …*

Students write out their version, then compare with their partner. Finally, you write the text on the board as they dictate it back to you.

Davis, P. and Rinvolucri, M. (1988) *Dictation*. Cambridge: Cambridge University Press.

Fanselow, J. (2010) *Try the Opposite*. Tokyo: Booksurge Pubs.

Fanselow, J. (2012) *Breaking Rules*. CreateSpace Independent Publishing Platform.

Shortening a Text

> A key feature of playfulness is willingness to take risks
> with the language. Literary texts are not sacred documents
> and there is nothing wrong in engaging with such texts.
> In fact, doing so gives students the chance to stretch their
> linguistic muscles and manipulate the language in new and
> creative ways.

In this activity, students are asked to shorten a well-known classic text. Choose and distribute a poem at about their proficiency level, and allow time for them to read it and note down any words they do not know. Discuss these with the whole class. Students then work in groups of four. Allocate different stanzas to different groups. They have to write a short summary of what their stanza is saying.

Still in groups of four, students will now try to shorten the poem without losing any of the essential message. For example, there are 24 lines in Wordsworth's poem *I wandered lonely as a cloud* below. Students have to reduce these to just 16 lines. They can only do this by removing complete lines. The lines they retain should connect together smoothly but do not need to retain the rhyme scheme of the original. Deciding on which lines to delete can be the focus of intense discussion which goes to the heart of what is most significant in the text.

Allow 15 minutes for students to work on the poem, then each group will join another group to discuss their two versions. How similar are they? Have they preserved the overall meaning?

In the same groups, now ask them to reduce their sixteen lines to just eight lines, still keeping intact as much of the original message as possible. Again they compare their versions with another group.

Make fair copies of the students' versions and put up a wall display (or add them to the class or school website). Students can be invited to add illustrations or photos at this stage.

A final step might be to ask students to reduce the poem to a haiku (see **14 Counting Syllables**) – just five syllables in line one, seven in line two and five in line three. For example:

daffodils dancing	*dancing daffodils*
in the breeze of memory	*by the lake so long ago –*
as I lie dozing	*they dance in my mind*

I wandered lonely as a cloud
William Wordsworth

I wandered lonely as a cloud
That floats on high o'er dales and hills,
When all at once I saw a crowd,
A host, of golden daffodils;
Beside the lake, beneath the trees,
Fluttering and dancing in the breeze.

Continuous as the stars that shine
And twinkle in the milky way,
They stretched in never-ending line
Along the margin of the bay:
Ten thousand saw I at a glance,
Tossing their heads in sprightly dance.

The waves beside them danced; but they
Outdid the sparkling waves in glee:
A poet could not but be gay
In such a jocund company!
I gazed, and gazed, but little thought
What wealth the show to me had brought:

For oft, when on my couch I lie,
In vacant or in pensive mood,
They flash upon that inward eye
Which is the bliss of solitude;
And then my heart with pleasure fills,
And dances with the daffodils.

36 Comparing Texts

> Developing a critical eye and a feel for the effective use of language can help in sharpening students' own written work. These are two simple ways of working with comparison and contrast.

Ask students to read these two poems carefully, noticing all the ways they are similar (number of lines, rhyming scheme, roughly the same meaning of lines, etc.), and how they are different (mainly vocabulary choice). Discuss the choice of vocabulary. Which seems more effective? Explain that one of these is a famous poem, the other is a made-up version. Which one is the original famous poem? (No checking on the Internet!) The original is B, written by Alfred Tennyson. Though both versions have the same rhyme scheme (AAA, BBB) text A contains awkward choices of vocabulary: *encircled, furrowed/crawls.*

A

He grasps the rock with
ruthless claws,
Close to the sun he writes his laws.
Encircled by the heavens, he soars.
The furrowed deep beneath
him crawls.
He scans the world from his
mountain halls.
Then, like a judgement day, he falls.

B

He clasps the crag with
crooked hands,
Close to the sun in lonely lands,
Ring'd with the azure world,
he stands
The wrinkled sea beneath
him crawls:
He watches from his mountain
walls
And, like a thunderbolt,
he falls

Faced with a single text, we often find it difficult to notice things about it. Faced with two texts, we immediately see things we might not otherwise have noticed. Students carefully note which features make these two poems below similar (both start the same way, both

74 | *Alan Maley's 50 Creative Activities*

are addressed to a lover, etc.) and which different (e.g. different subject matter, tone – gentle reminiscence/angry defiance, the Yeats is all about 'you', the other is all about 'me', verse structure and rhyme scheme, vocabulary choice, etc.). Ask students which poem they prefer and why.

When you are old and grey
and full of sleep
And nodding by the fire, take
down this book,
And in it read, and dream of
the soft look
Your eyes had once, and of
their shadows deep.

How many loved your
moments of glad grace,
And loved your beauty with love
false or true;
But one man loved the pilgrim
soul in you.
And loved the sorrows of your
changing face.

And bending down beside the
glowing bars
Murmur, a little sadly, how
love fled
And paced upon the mountains
overhead
And hid his face amid a cloud
of stars.
W.B. Yeats

When I am old and grey and full
of death
Caress me still and with your
breath
Assure me that I live.

Despite all proof of imminent
collapse
Contrive to bring relief, through
your belief
In permanence of a kind,
perhaps

When winter's light pales down
To dark and cold and void
Let us be gay in living
What we can't avoid.

Let death be sure
We will not let him gloat
But rather stuff his message
Down his throat!
A. Maley

Permutating Grammar

> Grammar is one of the pillars of any language. Yet one of
> the problems with teaching grammar is that it is not much
> fun. There are, fortunately, a number of ways to make
> grammar more enjoyable. This is just one of them.

The activity below offers students a way of doing grammar which is
enjoyable, creatively and aesthetically engaging and practical but which
does not carry a heavy load of grammatical terminology and analysis.

You need to find a sentence susceptible to multiple rearrangements of
the words. For example:

Nobody knows the woman he loves. or *It is all in the mind.*

Students work individually to produce as many permutations of this
sentence as possible. For example: *He knows the woman nobody loves.*
etc. Allow ten minutes for this.

When time is up, students form pairs and compare the sentences they
have found. They make a combined list, then continue searching for
more sentences. After a few more minutes, pairs join to make groups of
four, again pooling their sentences and continuing to write more.

Ask how many sentences each group has found. Write them on the
board, checking that they are grammatically acceptable. Are any
marginally acceptable, e.g. *Knows nobody he loves the woman*? Are
any of them meaningless, e.g. *The woman he nobody knows loves*?
You should end up with about 15 different acceptable sentences on
the board.

Now ask students to arrange the 15 or so sentences in an order which
will make a poem. There is an example below. If they find it difficult,
give them a clue: *Nobody...*, *He...*, *The woman...*, or show them the
first stanza below.

Nobody knows the woman he loves.
He knows nobody the woman loves.
The woman loves nobody he knows.

Nobody loves the woman he knows.
He knows nobody loves the woman.
The woman he knows loves nobody.

Nobody knows he loves the woman.
He knows the woman nobody loves.
The woman he loves knows nobody.

Nobody he knows loves the woman.
He loves the woman nobody knows.
The woman knows he loves nobody.

Nobody he loves knows the woman.
He knows the woman loves nobody.
The woman nobody knows – he loves.

You can extend the activity by having them write a short sentence after each line, beginning with *So...* e.g. *Nobody knows the woman he loves. So it's a secret.*

He knows nobody the woman loves. So he is not close to her. etc. This will help focus on the change of meaning which the permutation brings about, rather then merely on the mechanical manipulation.

You will notice that relative pronouns have been omitted from the text (quite correctly, of course). Ask students to go through the poem adding *that* and *who* where appropriate, e.g. *Nobody knows the woman **who** he loves. He knows nobody **that** the woman loves.* This shows the relationships in a more explicit way.

Norrington-Davies, D. (2016) *Teaching Grammar from Rules to Reasons: Practical Ideas and Advice for Working with Grammar in the Classroom.* London: Pavilion Publishing and Media Ltd.

Rinvolucri, M. (1985) *Grammar Games.* Cambridge: Cambridge University Press.

38 Mirror Words

> This activity is to encourage students to adopt a playful attitude to words. Words are infinitely interesting and can relate to each other in many different ways. This is just one idea for opening up an interest in vocabulary manipulation.

There are many words in English which mirror each other. That is, they can be read forwards or backwards. For example, *raw / war*. I call these mirror words. In this example, there is a perfect match – the letters are identical, and so are the sounds. There are other examples where the spelling does not match but the sound does, like *kill / lick*. Or where the spelling is identical but the sound is different, like *now / won*. But all of them qualify as mirror words.

You could start by explaining what mirror words are and giving a few examples, like *dog / god, fine / knife, rail / liar, etc.* Ask if anyone can think of any others. You might prompt by writing up a few words on the board and asking what the mirror word might be. For example: *team, evil, feel, etc.* which should produce *meat, live, leaf.* You will need enough for each student to have a different word.

Prepare two sets of cards. Set A consists of one half of a mirror word pair: *teach, kill, steam, evil, reef, eat, back, ban, top, feel, tap, raw, dear, saw, now, toll, poke, leak, seal, peel, ripe, teen, tame, bomb, stop, draw, stack, fine, noose, law, march, less, slope, pokes, cheap, kiss, stark, mask, trap.*

Set B consists of the matching words for those in Set A: *cheat, lick, meats, live, fear, tea, cab, nab, pot, leaf, pat, war, read, was, won, lot, cope, keel, lease, leap, pyre, neat, mate, mob, pots, ward, cats, knife, soon, wall, charm, sell, poles, scope, peach, sick, cast, scam, part.*

Divide the class into two groups, A and B. Make sure that there are equal numbers in each group. Hand out words from Set A to one group and from Set B to the other. Explain that students must look for their mirror word by circulating and asking other students. When they meet another student they should first say their word, then show it. The activity goes on until everyone has found their partner.

The pairs stay together and try to make an interesting sentence which contains both their words. For example, *If you teach, try not to cheat. When the leopard kills a deer, it licks the blood.* Let them share their sentences with other pairs.

Select some pairs of words which have a suggestive associative link, e.g. *cheat / teach; live / evil; back / cab; feel / leaf; seal / lease; sell / less; leak / keel; raw / war; mate / tame; noose / soon; law / wall; scam / mask; kiss / sick,* etc. Students can then use these to write short texts.

Make a wall display with the pairs of words. Encourage students to go on adding pairs of mirror words until the end of the course.

There is a whole range of other games you can play with words, for example, one letter substitution to form new words. For each of the following words, you are allowed either to cut one letter, add one letter or move the position of one or more letters. For example: *shame / same; slight / sight / sigh; gave / grave / brave; dog / god; decide / deride; smile / slime / miles / limes.* Students can try to write a two to three line poem using one set of the words you have generated. For example:

> I see his smile
> So full of slime –
> It makes me want
> To run a mile.

There are plenty of weblinks for those who catch the word bug and want to carry on outside class.

Crystal, D. (1998) *Language Play.* London: Penguin.

Espy, W. R. (1971) *The Game of Words.* London: Wolfe Publishing.

The object of these activities is to make students aware of the way English is in constant flux and to understand some of the processes involved. Along the way, they may well also acquire some interesting new words.

So how do new words come about? In this activity you can explore with students the answer to this question and give them the opportunity to coin some new English words of their own. You will need to allow at least two class hours for this: one for the discussion and one for the coining of new words.

Talk students through this list of some of the main ways new words are coined:

- Through borrowing, e.g. *barbecue* (Spanish), *sauna* (Finnish), *sushi* (Japanese)
- Through blends, e.g. *brunch* (a meal between breakfast and lunch), *smog* (smoke and fog)
- By making new compounds, e.g. *laptop, leapfrog, microwave*
- By using prefixes or suffixes, e.g. *multimedia, multi-tasking, supermarket, outsourcing*
- By using old words in new meanings, e.g. *crane* (from bird to machine), *mouse* (from animal to computer control), *surf* (verb, from water sport to computer search)
- By forming a new part of speech, e.g. *to parent, to obsess, to enthuse, a rave*
- From trademark names, e.g. *a hoover, a biro, i-pad, xerox, kleenex, band-aid, velcro, post-its, breathalyser, tupperware, google,* all proper names which have become common usages
- By clipping, e.g. *mike (microphone), sync (synchronize), exam (examination), petrol (petroleum), percent (-age)*
- By occupying vacant spaces in the sound system, e.g. **spum, *plute, *greff, *sleem*

- By occupying vacant spaces in the morphological system, e.g. *trendy* (adjective formed from noun), *gentrify* (make old houses fashionable), *tweetful** (describing someone who sends many tweets)
- By using acronyms, e.g. *UN (United Nations), EU (European Union), NGO (Non-governmental organization)*
- By using abbreviations, e.g. *asap (as soon as possible), aka (also known as), DIY (Do It Yourself).*

(* indicates a word which does not yet exist)

At the end of the first class, allocate one of the above devices to each pair of students. Before the next class they should try to find at least three examples of words created in this way. Give them a hint that there are many websites devoted to new words. As a class project, make a wall chart with numbered columns. Over the coming weeks, encourage students to add new words in the appropriate columns.

Give students a list of words, some of which are real English words, some which could be English words but which do not (yet) exist, and some which do not look or sound like English words at all. Do not allow dictionaries or phones at this stage. For example:

secular, cwybi, traduzzi, infra-block, punctilious, promb, xenophobia, binker, cable, mendacious, charcology, amphibious, lurgy, grimp, scrat, czetnakar, blarney, cottle, skeffing, kfessix, undermine, zdenka, chutle, intone, blooffer, insidious, burly

In groups, students decide if the words are real, could be real but don't exist or could not exist. After class discussion, students check in dictionaries.

'Words in Waiting.' As we can see above, the phonetic structure of English words is only partially realized. For example, we have the words *slam, slim, slum, slime,* but we do not have the potential words *slem, slerm, sloom, slume, slarm, slom, sleam, slame,* etc. We have the word *spoof,* but not the potential words *spife, sperf, spufe, speef, spoff,* etc. In groups, allow students ten minutes to think of as many possible new words as they can. The winning group is the one with the most 'new' words. For each invented new word, students then try writing a sentence which gives an idea of what it means.

Ayto, J. (1999) *20th Century Words.* Oxford: Oxford University Press.

http://public.oed.com/the-oed-today/recent-updates-to-the-oed/

40 The Long and the Short of It

> This is a disguised grammar activity. Rather than talking about the differences between simple, compound and complex sentences, it offers the possibility of growing a sentence as a hands-on experience. The idea is to start with a simple sentence and progressively to add elements to it until it is as long as possible.

You can introduce the topic of sentence length by asking students about writers they find easy or difficult to understand (in their own language as well as in English). What causes the difficulty? Difficult vocabulary? Difficult ideas? Unfamiliar cultural content? Difficult grammar – especially when sentences are too long? Explain that you are going to help them write a very long sentence. Then talk students through the following example, preferably by using slides to which you can add one item at a time and asking students the questions in brackets.

The young man felt sick. (Ask students the question: How sick?)

*The young man felt **very** sick.* (Just very sick?)

*The young man felt very sick **indeed**.* (What about his face? What was he wearing? When was that?)

*The **pale-faced** young man **in a tutu and tights** felt very sick indeed **later**.* (When was later?)

*The pale-faced young man in a tutu and tights felt very sick indeed later, **after eating**.* (What did he eat?)

*The pale-faced young man in a tutu and tights felt very sick indeed later, after eating **the meal**.* (What meal was that?)

*The pale-faced young man in a tutu and tights felt very sick indeed later, after eating the meal **the vicar's wife had cooked**.* (Who did she cook it for?)

*The pale-faced young man in a tutu and tights felt very sick indeed later, after eating the **special** meal the vicar's wife had cooked **for the theatre company**.* (When was that?)

*The pale-faced young man in a tutu and tights felt very sick indeed later, after eating the special meal the vicar's wife had cooked for the theatre company **when they visited the prison**.* (Why did they visit the prison?)

*The pale-faced young man in a tutu and tights felt very sick indeed later, after eating the special meal the vicar's wife had cooked for the theatre company when they visited the prison **to put on 'Murder in the Cathedral'**.* (When was that?)

*The pale-faced young man in a tutu and tights felt very sick indeed later, after eating the special meal the vicar's wife had cooked for the theatre company when they visited the prison to put on 'Murder in the Cathedral' **last summer**.* (Did anything memorable happen?)

*The pale-faced young man in a tutu and tights felt very sick indeed later, after eating the special meal the vicar's wife had cooked for the theatre company when they visited the prison to put on 'Murder in the Cathedral' last summer **during that terrible storm**.*

The students work in pairs or small groups. Give each group a simple sentence to work with. For example: *The man bit the dog. Peter married Jane. I like spaghetti. The student lost his laptop.* etc. Each pair or group now takes it in turns to add one element to the sentence to make it longer. This can be a word, a phrase or a clause. Each time they add an element, they need to write out the sentence (as in the example above). Set a time limit of about 15 minutes. Then ask each group to read out their sentence. Check the sentences are correct and discuss any errors. Which group has the longest (and correct) sentence? During feedback you may wish to highlight the devices used: pre-nominal modification, post-nominal modification, dependent and non-dependent clauses, adverbials, etc. but this is not necessary with all classes.

You could discuss whether writing ultra-long sentences is a help or a hindrance in making meaning clear. You could also do the activity in reverse by giving a very long sentence, and asking students to reduce it progressively by taking turns to remove one word or phrase at a time.

41   Onomatopoeia

> Most languages have a category of words which in some way mimic the sound of their meaning. (In English, *moo* is supposed to mimic the sound a cow makes.) These suggestions can help sensitize students to onomatopoeia while engaging in enjoyable activities which involve them in physical as well as cognitive and affective work.

You might begin by giving a couple of examples of sounds which represent animals: *cuckoo, baa*, etc. Ask students how these and other animal sounds are represented in their own languages. If you have a multilingual class, ask students from different languages to stand in a row – you give the sound in English, and each student then gives the equivalent in their own language.

Before the class, prepare small cards with onomatopoeic words written on them. Prepare five cards for each category below. (If you need help remembering, there are plenty of websites listing onomatopoeic words.)

You will need enough sets of these cards for every group of five students to have a set. Explain that such words are not random but can be grouped into different categories: animal sounds (*eyore*), sounds made by the human voice (*shriek*), by liquids (*gurgle*), by breaking (*smash*), by striking (*bang*), by metals (*squeak*). Here is one possible list of words grouped as above:

- Words representing animal sounds: *baa, buzz, chirp, cluck, coo, croak, cuckoo, growl, hiss, honk, hoot, miaow, moo, neigh, oink, quack, twitter, whinny, woof*
- Words representing human sounds: *burp, croak, gargle, gasp, giggle, groan, gurgle, hiccup, hiss, moan, mumble, munch, murmur, scream, shriek, shrill, sigh, slurp, sniff, snort, spit, wail, wheeze*
- Words for liquid sounds: *bubble, dribble, drip, drizzle, gurgle, gush, ooze, plop, slosh, splash, splat, splatter, spray, sprinkle, squash, squirt, squishy*

- Words for breaking noises: *burst, crack, crash, crunch, crush, slash, smash, snap, splinter, split, squash*
- Words for striking: *bang, bash, boom, bump, clap, clump, pat, slam, slap, splat, swat, tap, thump*
- Words for metallic sounds: *boing, clang, click, clonk, creak, ding-dong, jangle, jingle, ping, scrape, screech, tick-tock, ting-aling, tinkle, twang*

Divide the class into groups of five and give each group a set of the cards (mixed up). Allocate one category to each group (e.g. animal sounds, metallic sounds etc.). Students then have to go through all the cards and take out just the words that fit their category. They are allowed to consult dictionaries. Check the results in a feedback session. (Notice that some words, like *gurgle*, can fit in more than one category.)

Students can then do one or both of the following creative tasks:

Each group uses its words to create a vocal tapestry (see **16 Vocal Tapestry**). Each group member would have one or more words to repeat in different combinations to make a harmonious performance.

Groups use their category words to write a short onomatopoeic poem. There are many onomatopoeic poems on websites but it is better to show these examples after students have written their own to avoid plagiarism. Make a wall display or put the poems up on the class or school website.

> All languages have many more or less fixed expressions
> which capture wise observations about life. Proverbs and
> sayings are both highly culturally specific and universal.
> So this is an area of figurative language use worth
> exploring with students.

These activities are among many you can do using proverbs.

Print out cards or slips of paper with one half of a proverb (or a saying).
For example:

A	B
You can lead a horse to water but	*you can't make it drink.*
There's no smoke	*without fire.*
A stitch in time	*saves nine.*
People in glasshouses	*shouldn't throw stones.*
The grass is always greener	*on the other side of the fence.*
The early bird	*catches the worm.*
Don't put all your eggs	*in one basket.*
Don't count your chickens	*until they are hatched.*
Birds of a feather	*flock together.*
A watched pot	*never boils.*
Too many cooks	*spoil the broth.*

You need as many cards as there are students, i.e., for 20 students you
need 10 full proverbs divided into two. Divide the class into two equal
groups, A and B. Groups face each other on each side of the room.
The two lines meet and everyone tries to find the other half of their
proverb. Pairs then act out their proverb for others to guess. They
then read out their completed proverbs. They must also explain their
meaning. Discuss whether there are equivalent proverbs in the students'
own languages. For example, *Shallow streams make most noise* is the
Turkish equivalent of *Empty vessels make most noise*.

Just for fun, ask students to identify the full proverbs mixed up in the poem *Symposium* by Paul Muldoon, which starts:

> You can lead a horse to water but you can't make it hold
> its nose to the grindstone and hunt with the hounds.

You can use this as a lead-in to students writing their own mixed-up proverbs. Give them up to 50 popular proverbs. They then try to match different halves to create original proverbs, as in the poem. They are allowed to make small changes, as in *A watched pot spoils the broth.* or *Birds of a feather catch the worm.*

You can extend this activity further by making completely new proverbs or sayings. Make two sets of cards, both with evocative words or phrases. Here are some examples:

A	B
Death	helps heal
Revenge	the winner
A fish	too late
Love	swim uphill
Luck	needs a victim
A knife	waste time
A tortoise	empty grave

You can do this in two ways. Either give out the two sets of all the cards to groups. Students then try to make as many proverbs/sayings as they can. For example, *Death hates an empty grave.* Alternatively, put the cards in two separate boxes. Each student takes a card at random from each box. They then have to try to make a proverb/saying by finding a way of connecting the two cards. For example: *Luck / swim uphill*, might lead to: *Luck cannot help you swim uphill.*

However, a word of caution. Though proverbs are part of the texture of the language, they are relatively rarely used. And when they are, we rarely complete them. For example, *Too many cooks...* is enough to trigger reference to *...spoil the broth.* It is as if we need to know them so as not to need to use them! People who overuse proverbs sound odd – and a bit boring.

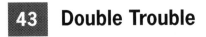

43 Double Trouble

> Vocabulary is highly organized in many interlocking sub-
> systems, though these are complex. This activity will look
> in more detail at one of the systematic lexical networks,
> namely what some linguists call *doublets* or *binomials*.

Doublets are two words or phrases joined by *and, or, to* or *by*. For
example: *bread and butter, fish and chips, aches and pains, love or
money, friend or foe, back to front, top to bottom, more or less, blow by
blow, etc.* Decide on a list of about 50 doublets. Here is a possible list
but you can easily choose alternatives, there are plenty to choose from.
Prepare cards with a doublet on each.

*aches and pains, all or nothing, back and forth, bigger and better, bit by
bit, black and blue, black and white, checks and balances, cut and dried,
dead or alive, dos and don'ts, fair and square, fast and loose, fish and
chips, heads or tails, health and safety, high and dry, high and low, knife
and fork, life and death, little by little, now or never, null and void, nuts
and bolts, odds and ends, one to one, open and shut, over and over, part
and parcel, peace and quiet, pins and needles, rise and fall, rough and
ready, safe and sound, short and sweet, side by side, song and dance,
sooner or later, spick and span, sugar and spice, thick and thin, through
and through, time and again, tit for tat, tooth and nail, toss and turn,
ups and downs, win or lose.*

Introduce the notion of doublets by giving a common example, like *fish
and chips*. Do students know of any other pairs of words like this? They
will probably suggest *bread and butter, salt and pepper*, etc.

Distribute a doublet card to each student. They circulate and try to
convey their doublet to others by miming it. In feedback with the class
discuss the difficulties they encountered.

Prepare two sets of cards. Set A will have the first half of a doublet
(e.g. *health and…*). Set B will have the second half of the doublets

(e.g. *safety*). Divide the class into two groups, A and B, and distribute the corresponding sets of cards. Students then circulate until they have found the full doublet. Again discuss the activity and any special difficulties.

Draw students' attention to the different ways these fixed collocations are structured. These include:

- Two near-identical items: *aches and pains, blow by blow, fun and games, loud and clear, round and round, safe and sound, spick and span*, etc.
- Two opposite items: *give and take, life and death, love or money, on and off, to and fro, up and down, win or lose*, etc.
- Two items which are semantically related: *accident and emergency, an arm and a leg, egg and bacon, head and shoulders, pen and pencil, tooth and nail, whisky and soda*, etc.
- Two alliterative or rhyming items: *doom and gloom, fair and square, hard and fast, high and dry, odds and ends, past and present, prim and proper*, etc.

Students then work in groups of four. Distribute 10 randomly-chosen doublet cards to each group. They have five minutes to arrange them according to whether they are identical, opposites, associated or alliterative/rhyming. Groups then report back to the class.

For the next class, ask students to collect more of these doublets for sharing and discussion.

Set a writing task to be done outside class. They should write a short poem (four or five lines only) using doublets. For example:

Up and down	Fast and loose
Round and round.	Profit and loss
At last we're home	Down and out
Safe and sound.	Because of the boss.

You can use a search engine to find "Lexical doublets".

44 Body Language

It is remarkable that there are so many words connected with the parts of the human body, offering a rich vocabulary resource. The object of this activity is to raise awareness of the usefulness of words and expressions derived from body parts so that students can look out for them, especially in reading.

Start by offering a few examples on the board of how the word *head* crops up in expressions in English. For example:

a bear with a sore head, a head for heights, a head start, a headhunter, a headless chicken, from head to toe, go head to head, hard-headed, he's a big- / an egg-head, head and shoulders (above), head off (their manoeuvre), head on (collision), head over heels, headlong, headstrong, hot-headed, I can't get my head round it, keep your head down, off the top of my head, off your head, pig-headed, the head waiter, turning the argument on its head, (won) by a short head

Are any of these kinds of expression found in the students' own languages? Explain that *head* is not the only body part which is enlisted for extended use. Then divide the class into groups of four. Give each group two examples of expressions using other parts of the body. For example:

- Hair: *keep your hair on, splitting hairs*
- Eye: *an eye for an eye (a tooth for a tooth), eye to eye (don't see)*
- Back: *back to front, get off my back*
- Knee(s): *knee-high to a grasshopper, weak-kneed*
- Foot/feet: *feet on the ground, sure-footed*

Each group then tries to find at least three more expressions using their body part and reports back to the class. They may use dictionaries, phones or tablets for this. Finally, ask the class to find any expressions based on: *arm(s), belly, cheek(s), chest, ear(s), elbow(s), fingers, heart, mouth, neck, nose, shoulder(s), stomach.*

Prepare a large wallchart or a page on the class website with spaces for each body part. Groups then record the expressions they have discovered in the appropriate spaces. For artistically-inclined classes, the chart could be an outline of a human body so that expressions can be attached to the corresponding place on the body. Ideally, this should be an on-going activity where any new usages encountered in reading, online, in advertisements, etc. should be recorded, on the wallchart or on the class website.

To round off this session, give the students this poem to read. In groups of five they then prepare a performance of the poem (see **25 Performing Texts**).

Heart to heart
Don't look down your nose at me, please –
When you catch my eye, I go weak at the knees.
You're head and shoulders there above little me,
But I'm head over heels in love with you, you see.
Don't laugh at me behind my back
Or treat me like a one-eyed jack.
I know your fingers are in many pies
But let my heart give yours – a surprise.

If this activity catches the imagination of students, you can extend it by investigating other areas rich in figurative usage, such as animals (*the lion's share*, etc.), nautical terms (*all at sea*, etc.), the weather (*a fair wind*, etc.).

45 How Frequent?

> One obvious criterion for vocabulary selection is frequency. However, teaching these words may be more problematic than we expect. The more common a word, the larger the number of meanings it has. And it is often the more uncommon words which stick in the memory.

This activity is one way of exploring creatively the frequency of vocabulary in English. Before the lesson, prepare about 100 cards with frequent *content* words on them and put them in a box.

Start off by asking the class which is the most frequent word in the English language. Be prepared for some mighty strange ideas! (Most word counts put *the* at the top for frequency.)

Now ask students individually to write down what they think are the 10 most frequent words in English (no phones or tablets allowed!). They then join with a partner. They share their lists and have to arrive at an agreed list of 10. This will involve making compromises about which words to cut.

Each pair then joins with another pair to form groups of four. They again share their lists and have to come to agreement about which will be their final list of 10 most frequent words. In a class feedback session collect the ideas from each group and try to construct a list the whole class can agree on. Students write this list down.

In groups again, students are allowed to add another 10 most frequent words to their lists. They must all agree on their new list. Groups share the new words with the class again. Each group now has 20 words. The list might look something like this (though it may look rather different!):

a, and, are, can, do, have, he, I, in, is, it, not, of, that, the, they, to, was, with, you

Now allow students to check word frequency using their phones, etc. They can search 'most frequent English words'. How do their word lists compare with those they find on one of the search engines? Discuss their findings. One thing to emerge will be that the most frequent words, whether in spoken or written language, are function words. But to communicate, we need to have something to communicate about: we need content words.

Tell groups that they may now remove five of the words from their list, and add five new words which are frequent content words – nouns, verbs or adjectives. This might leave a group with a list something like this:

and, are, can, do, get, good, have, I, in, is, it, love, not, say, the, they, to, want, was, you

Now each group has to use the words in their list to write as many sentences as possible. Tell students they may use all the forms of a word (*say, says, said, saying*, etc.). So they might form sentences like: *I love you – you are good to me. You said I was good. You want to have love.* etc. Let them try for at least five minutes. It will soon be obvious that they can only say a very limited number of things.

Groups are now allowed to draw a maximum of five words from the box you prepared earlier. But they have to draw the cards one at a time. Before drawing a new card, groups must have exhausted all the possibilities of the previous one. Finally, they try to write a short text, prose or poem, using the sentences they have generated.

Students benefit greatly from the constant manipulation of words. They become more aware of key features of the English lexicon: function words, content words, the limitations on usage, etc. They also gain from the intense discussion about the relative frequency and usefulness of words.

46 Alliteration and Assonance

> Among the most frequently used literary devices are *alliteration* and *assonance*. Both are essentially using repetition to achieve an effect. Alliteration involves repeating a consonant sound at the beginnings (and sometimes in the middle) of words. Assonance is the repetition of a vowel sound.

Explain what assonance and alliteration are and give examples from the wide range of domains in which they are used, apart from literature. For example:

- Book titles: *A Tale of Two Cities, Peter Pan, Pride and Prejudice*
- TV shows: *I Love Lucy, Sesame Street*
- Films: *Charlie and the Chocolate Factory, King Kong, La La Land, Pink Panther, Red River*
- Cartoon characters: *Barnacle Bill, Bugs Bunny, Donald Duck*
- Celebrity names: *Janis Joplin, Kim Kardashian, Marilyn Monroe*
- Newspaper headlines: *Crew Capsize Catamaran, President's Perks Prove Perjury*
- Product names: *Coca-Cola, PayPal, PowerPoint, Volkswagen, YouTube*

There are also many words which exploit these features: *claptrap, flipflop, hip-hop, humdrum, knickknack, ping pong, shilly-shally, ship-shape, singsong, slapdash, slipshod, tip-top.*

Hold a class discussion about the way alliteration and assonance function. Discuss why they are so prevalent. (Partly because they make the language more memorable. That is why they are much used in product names and advertising slogans. Perhaps also because our ears like to hear the repetition of sounds.) Ask students to collect as many examples from all these categories and bring them to the next class.

For the next class you will need to prepare some specifications like these providing basic information for students to work on:

- A newspaper headline: This is a story about a baby who killed a crocodile with its feeding bottle.
- A food product name: This is a new type of chocolate which has the flavour of celery.
- An invention: This is an invention to stop umbrellas blowing inside out in the wind.
- A health product: This is a system for giving up smoking using an extract from horse manure.
- A food product name: This is a new kind of pizza using nuts only.
- A book title: This is an autobiography of a man who lived on an island infested with poisonous snakes for 10 years.
- A book title: This is a novel about a girl who turns into a man every night and has adventures.
- A film title: This is a film about a spy who works for five different countries at the same time.

Discuss the items students have brought. Then tell them they will be developing some items of their own which use alliteration/assonance. Allocate the categories to groups of four. For each category, students should write a headline, product name etc., which uses alliteration/assonance. For example, the nut pizza might be: *Pecans, Peanuts and Pistachio Pizza*. The baby and the crocodile might be: *Baby Gives a Lot of Bottle to Croc*.

Then discuss results and prepare a wall display of the best examples.

Tell students that alliteration was a central feature of Anglo-Saxon poetry which did not rhyme but had special rules involving alliteration. Every line was divided into two equal parts, each with two main beats. The first three beats all had to alliterate, the fourth did not. For example, *The **dark deeps** / **down under** us.*

Write up some theme words on the board: *the moon, rain, a storm, money,* etc. The same groups of four choose a theme word and try to write two lines of Anglo-Saxon verse based on their theme. After about 15 minutes, groups share what they have written by reading it aloud. As homework or in the next class, they can add to their poem.

47 Welcome to Mrs Malaprop

> Mrs Malaprop was the linguistically anarchic character in Sheridan's *The Rivals*. Her bizarre use of inappropriate words led to such usages acquiring the name *malapropisms*. A malapropism is any word that is wrongly or accidentally used in place of a similar-sounding, correct word.

Essentially, this is an activity to encourage students to engage with vocabulary in an original and unthreatening way. Some of the words which emerge will be unusual but there is no suggestion that all these words should be learned. Rather, the activity helps students to focus on the meanings of words which will be useful by making them more salient. The element of humour can also contribute to vocabulary retention.

Give a few examples of malapropisms: *The Misery (Ministry) of Education; The French Revelation (Revolution); There were lots of old acorns (icons) in the church; They were all members of a futility (fertility) cult; This is a very hysterical (historical) building.* etc.

Then write up on the board a number of words which might be confused. For example: *Celt, fertility, futility, kilt, lawyer, lemon, liar, melon, riot, rite, room, savoury, slavery, womb,* etc. You need about 30 words. Make sure they are mixed up. In pairs, students first have to find the words which could be confused, e.g. *liar/lawyer*. They then have to create sentences where each word is used inappropriately. For example, *Can I have a slice of melon in my tea? / That lemon I had for lunch was so sweet.* Share the examples with the whole class, and discuss any new words which have cropped up.

Give students this poem, which lists some possible malapropisms:

How can we tell –
Sedation from sedition?
Mass destruction from mass distraction?
Aptitude from attitude?
Fertility from futility?
Feudal from foetal?
Compliance from complaints?
Ecumenical from economical?
Lethargy from liturgy?
A clown from a clone?
Unanimous from anonymous?
Poetry from pottery?
Elegance from eloquence?
A creditor from a predator?
And words from worlds?

Students list any words they are unsure of, then check their meanings in a dictionary.

Then distribute a list of words which have potential for generating malapropisms. Students work in pairs to come up with possible malapropisms based on these words, for example, *acquisition – accusation*. In these examples, some answers are suggested in brackets, though these would obviously not be given out to the students:

a ferry (a fairy); a moral (a mural); acquisition (accusation); archery (artery); assets (acids); collusion (collision); comic (cosmic); conversation (conservation); desperate (disparate); drama (trauma); ghostly (ghastly); horse (hearse); melody (malady); midges (midgets); parrot (carrot)

Students then use about 10 of their pairs of words to create their own poem based on the model of the one provided earlier.

Once again, make sure there is time for discussion about these words and their meanings, and arrange for students' poems to be displayed as an exhibition.

E: Hands-on Activities

These activities all engage learners in using language through making things with their hands.

Construction Site

Usually, students do not get much chance to move around, to use their bodies for self-expression or to use their hands to make something. Some students whose learning style preference is for the physical manipulation of things are disadvantaged by the emphasis on intellectual kinds of learning in most classrooms. Including some activities which cater for these types of student may also help other students to discover hidden talents.

For this activity you will need to divide the class into groups of four to six students. Groups larger than six usually means some of them are simply passengers, leaving the work to the others. Each group will be given exactly the same set of materials: eight large file cards, 20 paper clips, 10 elastic bands, four thick, coloured markers.

Before you give out the materials, you will need to explain what students are to do. Their task is to use the materials to build a 'structure', which could be an architectural model for a building. You can tell them that this is a competition between architects for a distinguished, international prize! But there are rules:

They must use *all* the materials.

They can bend but not fold the cards.

The structure must be completed in 20 minutes.

The structure will be judged according to three criteria: height (the tallest is best), sturdiness (the structure must not wobble or fall over easily) and artistic appearance (it must look attractive or innovative in some way).

You may want to remind students about the kind of language they will need to use: Polite requests – *Can you please ..., Could you ..? Would you mind ...*; Imperatives – *Please pass me ..., Put it ... Hold this ...*; Suggestions – *Why don't we ...? How about ...? We could..., Let's try ...*; Expressing preferences – *I like X better than Y, It looks nicer with ..., I think it's better to ... .*

When groups have finished their structures, go round to each group and note down a mark out of 10 for each aspect of the construction – height, sturdiness and attractiveness. Add up the scores and declare the winner. If possible, ask students to make a display of their work, giving a name to their constructions and taking photographs of their finished work.

You can, of course, vary the rules, for example, by allowing students to cut or fold the cards, or allowing the use of a paper stapler. You might also want to explore other kinds of material for similar construction tasks. One possibility is Lego, which is easily available in a multiplicity of kits. Another is to use the Cuisenaire rods associated with The Silent Way. These can either be used to make a picture or structure, or to illustrate the events in a story. You might also wish to experiment with Plasticine. Alternatively, each group is given a set of odd objects – buttons, pieces of cloth, socks, stones, leaves, etc. From this they must make an artwork – a sculpture, or a piece of installation art (see **49 Installation Art**).

You can extend the activity by adding a writing task. Each group should write instructions for making their construction. Groups exchange instructions and then do the task again, this time using the instructions to make another group's construction. As you (and they) will discover, this is fiendishly difficult to do but it will offer plenty more opportunities for discussion as they attempt to replicate their original process.

Another way to extend this into a writing activity is to ask them to write a publicity piece (decide how long you want this to be but I suggest not more than 10–15 lines). This should extol the qualities of the construction for a prospective buyer or sponsor.

Installation art aims to make us see familiar things in a fresh light by 'framing' them as art. Some assemblages of objects can be very moving and help us to see the world in a new way. Installation art lends itself well to language teaching: it is easy to make and there is a lot which can be said or written about it.

Before starting the activity, conduct a discussion session to find out how much students already know about installation art. Alternatively, before the class, ask them to do a web-search to find out as much as they can about it – and to report back in class. Discuss some key questions: Is this really art? How far should it be objects as they are found, like an unmade bed, and how much does it involve conscious, artistic re-arrangement to enhance the effect?

Ask students to bring to class five interesting-looking leaves and five smallish stones. They work in groups of three or four. Their task is to arrange the leaves and stones on a flat surface so as to create a piece of installation art. (As an alternative to leaves and stones, you could use many other kinds of object: medicine bottles, opened envelopes, shoes, cutlery, buttons, umbrellas, matchboxes, etc. But you will need to make sure each group has the same number of objects. This is a form of *knolling*, where similar kinds of objects are arranged on a flat surface for visual effect.)

Students do not have to use all the material but they can add more leaves or stones if they wish. Allow enough time for them to consider many options and to come to agreement (preferably in English). They should then decide on a title for their piece – the more striking or humorous, the better.

Tell students their work will be displayed as part of an exhibition. They will have to write a short paragraph to describe and promote their work. This will be placed next to their installation, along with the title. One person is then chosen as the spokesperson for the group. Students circulate to view each installation in turn. They read the texts, listen to the spokesperson, and ask questions or make comments. At the end, groups vote for the best, most striking or interesting or artistic installation. Groups cannot vote for their own piece.

Make sure that each installation piece is photographed so that there is a class record of the work produced. If possible, print out copies of the pictures and make a catalogue of the exhibition as a whole.

The installations can be the basis for other kinds of writing, including haiku, short prose poems, advertisements for a product, a newspaper review of the whole exhibition (very favourable or very critical).

In a follow-up class, help students to set up a debate focused on the role of art in society. Some possible topics would be:

- Modern art is a load of rubbish.
- There is no place for real art in our consumer society.
- 'Art is for the people.' (Joseph Stalin)
- There is no such thing as 'high art' or 'low art'. There is only good or bad art.

If you need help with organizing a debate, there are plenty of weblinks available.

Carey, J. (2006) *What good are the Arts?* London: Faber.

Perry, G. (2014) *Playing to the Gallery.* London: Penguin.

This is another activity involving physical as well as mental and emotional elements. Making a collage can be a social, collaborative process which involves coming to agreement about elements in response to an aesthetic stimulus.

You will need to prepare large sheets (60 × 60 cm) of thick paper (sugar paper, manila or thin cardboard are suitable). You need enough sheets for one per group of four students. You will also need glue, scissors, and some markers. For the collage materials, you can bring in lots of old colour magazines or catalogues. Alternatively, ask students to bring in pieces of old coloured cloth, buttons, leaves, etc. – the more, the better.

Explain what a collage is: a picture made of very small pieces of paper, cloth or other material, like shells or buttons, stuck on to a backing of paper to form a picture. Students will be making a collage in groups of four. This will then form part of an art exhibition.

Choose a poem or other short text which is highly visual, as in the example below. Here a poem is used as the stimulus but it could equally be a piece of emotive music (see **22 Moved by Music**), a newspaper article or a story.

Read the text below aloud, then give out copies. This will be the stimulus for the collage students will make.

The Panther
Year after year the bars go pacing past,
till in the end his very brain is blind.
With eyes wide open, all he sees at last
is bars, bars, bars, and emptiness behind.

And as he pads his cage with supple grace,
tracing his tiny circle, round and round,

a force goes turning, dancing round a place
in which a mighty will stands dumb and bound.

Sometimes the curtain briefly moves away.
An image enters, flickers past his eyes,
speeds through the waiting body, finds its way
straight to the heart; and dies.

(Translation of Rilke's *Panter. The Panther* by Michael Swan)

Groups now need to organize themselves. First they decide which words, phrases or images are most striking in the poem. What kind of a picture will they make? Representational or abstract? Who will sketch in the outline on the paper? Who will cut up the coloured paper or cloth into small pieces and put it in piles according to colour? Who will do the pasting? (It is better to lay out the pieces on the outline before actually sticking them. This allows for changes to be made.) Who will be in charge and make sure that the whole surface of the collage is covered in the most effective way?

When they have finished, groups should write an original title (**not** *Panther*). For example, *Exile from the forest...* or *Enslavement of the spirit*, etc. They then write a short paragraph which will appear next to the collage in the exhibition. This paragraph is to give visitors more information about the subject. For example, *The picture represents the idea of imprisonment and exile. Though it is based on Rilke's famous poem about a panther in a cage, it is also symbolic of the imprisoned soul in all of us. Note the use of dark colours to represent...* etc. Encourage students to be as imaginative as possible in writing this paragraph.

Finally, organize the exhibition. Half the groups (A) stand by their collages and answer questions from the other half (B). A and B then change places. This allows for plenty of interaction and repetition. If possible, invite other classes or visitors like parents to come to the exhibition. Make sure there are photographs so that there is a permanent record.

Index

Printed in the United States
By Bookmasters